AF423354

عقيـــلة الخيـــال
Muse's Reverie

عقيلة الخيال
Muse's Reverie

KAPH
ART BOOKS FROM THE ARAB WORLD
كتـب الفـن مـن العالـم العربـي

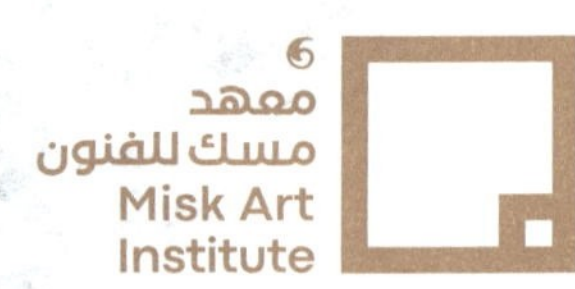

معهد
مسك للفنون
Misk Art
Institute

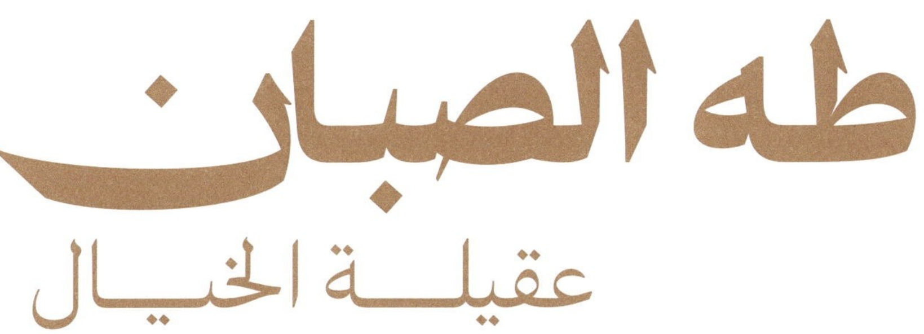

Taha Alsabban
Muse's Reverie

Exhibition Catalog | Solo Series

سلسلة المعارض الفردية
Solo Series

بسمة الشثري، مدير عام إدارة التقييم الفني وكبير القيمين الفنيين
Basma Alshathry, Director of Curatorial Department and Chief Curator

The Kingdom of Saudi Arabia is amidst a flourishing cultural era. As the art scene rapidly expands, it is of paramount importance, as custodians of culture, to document notable works of influential artists and their invaluable contributions.

In alignment with this role, Misk Art Institute presents the Solo Series; a significant milestone in the institute's cultural journey. Through this series, we aim to highlight pioneering Saudi artists who have played vital roles in shaping the local art scene. Each exhibition in this series offers a unique opportunity to delve deeply into the artistic journey of these influential figures, unraveling specific facets of their creative practice. Through the preservation of this artistic heritage, we strive to develop a nuanced comprehension of the artists' visual language and artistic aptitude.

The inaugural edition of the Solo Series pays homage to and showcases two pioneering Saudi artists, Taha Alsabban and Yousef Jaha. Misk Art Institute is committed to promoting artists and fostering the growth of the Saudi art scene. These exhibitions serve as essential archives that safeguard the artworks for present and future generations to explore and draw inspiration from. By preserving this artistic heritage, we aim to contribute to the perpetual growth and enrichment of the art scene, ensuring its vibrancy and relevance for years to come.

أخـذت الثقافة والفنون حيـزاً بيـن جوانب الازدهار التـي تشـهدها المملكـة العربيـة السـعودية، وفـي نمط متناغـم وبوتيرة متسـارعة بشـكل إيجابي يمرّ قطـاع الفنون والثقافـة في زمنية فارقـة؛ وفي هذا السـياق وانطلاقاً من واجبنـا الاجتماعي في حماية ثقافتنـا بتوثيقهـا بشـتى أشـكالها، يسـاهم معهـد مسـك للفنون فـي توثيق عمـل روّاد الفـن البصري في المملكـة العربية السـعودية ومسـيرتهم الفنية.

تشـكل سلسـلة المعارض الفردية التـي يطلقها المعهد خطـوة مهمة فـي مسـيرته، حيـث تسـلّط الضوء على مجموعة من روّاد الفن السـعودي الذين كان لهـم بالـغ الأثـر فـي تشـكيل المشـهد الفني في المملكة؛ ويأتي كُل معرض من هذه السلسـلة مقدماً فرصـة للتعمّق فـي التجربـة الفنية لهـؤلاء الفنانين، وكاشـفاً عـن تفاصيل ممارسـتهم الإبداعيـة ولغتهم البصرية والتشـكيلية.

يأتـي المعرضان الفرديان في أولى نسـخ هذه السلسـلة باثنين مـن روّاد الفن السـعودي هما طه الصبان ويوسـف جاها إبرازاً لجهودهما في المشهد الفنـي، وتحقيقاً لـدور المعهد في حماية الجهود المؤثـرة فـي حيوية هـذا القطـاع، لتكون انطلاقةً لسلسـلة تعزّز من نمو المشهد الفني وتعمل بمثابة أرشيف يقدّم الأعمـال الفنيـة الماضيـة للأجيـال الحاضرة والقادمة.

عقيلــــة الخيـــال
Muse's Reverie

آرام العجاجي وندى العرادي
Aram Alajaji and Nada Alaradi

With a career spanning over fifty years, Taha Alsabban stands as a pioneer and a luminary whose exploration of place, societal intricacies, and heritage positioned him as a preeminent figure in the Saudi art scene. Most known for his depictions of traditional architecture of Saudi cities, his distinctive painting style has gained him international recognition.

Muse's Reverie features forty-five paintings by Alsabban that highlight his exploration of the connections between women, tradition, time, and history, within the Saudi landscape. This exhibition sheds light on a crucial yet underexamined theme—the portrayal of women across various realms and identities.

Alsabban's oeuvre offers a glimpse into Saudi Arabia's cultural past, preserving the interwoven ties of place, people, and society through time. Delving into the artist's practice, we uncover the evolution of his distinctive style. Early in his career, Alsabban drew inspiration and guidance from pioneering Saudi artist Abdulhalim Radwi, who encouraged him to explore local themes and supported him in exhibiting his work extensively.

Alsabban progressed in his career and displayed his dedication to fostering the growth of talented female artists. He arranged exhibitions featuring female artists

يُعد طه الصبان رائداً من رواد الفن التشكيلي بمسيرةٍ تجاوزت الخمسـين عاماً، إذ تميّـز باستكشـافه وبحثه في المـكان والتعقيدات المجتمعية والتراث، وهو ما جعل منه شخصية بارزة في مشهد الفن السعودي، واشتهر برسـمه الإبداعي للهندسة المعمارية التراثية للمدن في المملكة العربية السـعودية، ما أذاع صيته ومنحـه الاعتـراف المحلـي والدولي. يضـم معرض «عقيلـة الخيـال» 45 لوحة مـن أعمال الصبان التي تسلط الضوء علـى الروابـط بيـن المرأة والتقاليـد والزمن والمشاهد الجماليـة فـي المملكة العربيـة السـعودية، كما يسـلط الضوء على أعمال الفنان من خـلال تقديـم فكرة مهمة لم تُطـرح مسـبقاً، وهي رسـمه للنسـاء عبر مختلف العوالم والهويات.

تقـدِّم أعمـال الفنـان طـه الصبان لمحةً عن الماضـي الثقافـي للمملكة العربيـة السـعودية، وحفـظ الروابـط بيـن المـكان والنـاس والمجتمع، ومـن خـلال التعمـق فـي أسـلوب الفنـان نلاحظ تطـوّره المتميـز. ففـي بدايـة حياتـه المهنيـة كان الفنان السعودي الرائـد عبد الحليم رضـوي ملهماً لـه، وهـو مـن شـجَّعه على استكشاف الأفكار المحليـة ودعمه للتوسـع فـي عـرض أعماله. ومع ازدهار حيـاة الصبـان المهنيـة، لـم يتخلَّ هو في المقابـل عـن تشـجيع الفنانـات الواعدات إذ أقام لهن معارض ومنحهنّ الدعم المالي، وأنشأ «جائزة طه الصبان للفنـون الجميلة للفنانـات الواعدات».

embedded within Alsabban's themes of women's place in society, cultural celebrations, and their relationship to the natural environment.

Centered on the intimate realm of womanhood and motherhood within domestic life, the spotlight falls on women's influential presence at the heart of society. Through abstract portraits that emphasize feminine elements, such as braids, traditional dresses, and the relationship between a mother and her child, Alsabban takes the subject into an intimate, private context allowing their feminine essence to emanate.

Beyond domestic life, Alsabban captures community, culture, and togetherness through celebrations. His artistic exploration includes the use of various materials, leading to the creation of a textured base for his paintings. In certain heavily textured works, the artist's skillful use of line alludes to the intricate ornamentation often found in traditional homes. In other paintings, the subtle incorporation of symbols of local architecture, such as the *rawasheen*, establishes a strong sense of place. Additionally, many of his works evoke a sense of nostalgia through their soft and dreamlike qualities. Regardless of Alsabban's chosen stylistic approach, the vibrant colors, clothing, and atmosphere convey the dynamism of the festivities. Alsabban skillfully captures the quieter moments of gatherings amidst the celebrations, where women are depicted in relaxed settings, engaged in conversations, or immersed in shared readings.

Alsabban's vivid paintings of women engaged in bustling market scenes bring the essence of community to life. Within these works, his compositions are filled with females grouped together in a public setting often holding baskets. Despite the bold use of purples, yellows, and greens, Alsabban's paintings are filled with vitality and joy, capturing the energy of market

أسَّس الصبان أسلوباً يتميز بتصوير أشخاص وهياكل ومبانٍ ممدودة، وهذا الأسلوب الفريد هو ما يميِّز أعماله ويضفي عليها إحساس الخيال والمرونة ويعبر فيها حدود الأزمنة، وبفنِّه المتفرِّد بألوانه وأدواته، يبني الصبان علاقته بمحيطه بدمجه للعناصر غير التقليدية مثل الرمل والأقمشة النسائية مع الأدوات التقليدية مثل الألوان الزيتية والأكريليك. كما تفيض لوحاته بسطوع السماوي والأخضر والأحمر، معبرةً عن القوة والتألّق، وتظهر جرأته في الألوان بطريقة عفوية، وغالباً ما تعكس حالته العاطفية في ذلك الوقت. وتُبرز علاقة الإيقاع وتدرجات الألوان في لوحاته السمات المميزة لكلِّ عنصر تركيبي؛ كما يحرص على الحفاظ على التراث الحجازي والسعودي برسم العديد من اللوحات التي تعبِّر عن حفلات الزفاف والمناظر الطبيعية المحلية والملابس التقليدية والمجوهرات، وفي هذا الجزء من أعماله يبرز استخدامه لأدوات كالأقمشة والمجوهرات.

ويُعد حضور المرأة فكرةً متجلية في أعمال الصبان، ويمثل رمزاً لأدوارها في المجتمع، وتأثيرها الكبير على الفنان، ولا تظهر في أعماله كمجرَّد موضوع بل هي مصدر إلهام يعكس الثقافة الاجتماعية المحيطة به، وفي لوحاته المعمارية التي لا تناقش المرأة كموضوع، فنلاحظ ظهورها بتلميحات مثل دمج الأقمشة النسائية كعلامات على تأثيرها، ويأتي هذا المعرض مجسداً المفاهيم والدلالات التي تشكِّل جزءاً لا يتجزأ من أفكار الصبان حول مكانة المرأة في المجتمع والموروث الثقافي وعلاقتها بالبيئة الطبيعية المحيطة بها.

إن تصويره لعالم المرأة يُبرز تأثيرها على المجتمع، وقد عمل الصبان على ذلك من خلال التصوير التجريدي الذي يبرز عناصر تُعبِّر عن المرأة، مثل ضفائر الشعر والملابس التقليدية والعلاقة بين الأم وطفلها، وغيرها من العناصر التي تُبرز دور المرأة الاجتماعي.

and offered them financial support through the *Taha Alsabban Award for Promising Female Artists.*

Alsabban cultivated a distinctive style characterized by elongated figures, structures, and buildings. This unique approach infuses his work with a dreamlike quality, creating a sense of fluidity and transcending the constraints of time. Fearlessly experimenting with colors and materials, Alsabban builds on his relationship with his surroundings by incorporating unorthodox elements such as sand and fabric from women's clothing with more traditional mediums of oil and acrylic. His paintings burst with bright blues, greens, and reds, asserting strength and radiance. While many of his works are monochromatic, Alsabban's choice of colors arises spontaneously, often reflecting his emotional state at the time. The interplay of tones and shades within his color palette accentuate the unique characteristics of each element in the composition. Through his mixed-media paintings, Alsabban preserves the rich heritage of Saudi culture, depicting diverse subjects such as marriage ceremonies, local landscapes, traditional clothing, and jewelery.

Throughout Alsabban's body of work, female figures are a heavily reoccurring motif. They carry pivotal and evocative symbols that signify their relationship to the cities they are situated within. From his early works to his most recent, the profound impact of women in his life remains a constant thread. The influence of women resonates deeply within his work, rather than mere subjects, they are a source of inspiration that reflect the life and culture within his community. In his architectural paintings where the female subject is not explicitly portrayed, Alsabban incorporates fabric from women's dresses into the composition as a testament to their enduring influence. Through these introspective depictions, *Muse's Reverie* explores layers of meaning and significance

يصور الفنان المرأة في محيطها الأسري ويركز على دورها كأم. والذي يبرز أثرها وأهميتها في المجتمع. وتجمع ممارسته الفنية العديد من المواد المختلفة التي تهيئ لعمله قاعدة ملموسة ومتميزة. إذ تتميَّز بعض أعماله المنسوجة برسومات تتضمن زخارف ونقوشاً للمنازل التقليدية، وفي لوحاته الأخرى يدمج الفنان رموزاً من العمارة المحلية كالرواشين، بينما تعبر الكثير من أعماله عن الحنين إلى الماضي من خلال العديد من السمات الحالمة. وبغض النظر عن الأسلوب الفني الذي اختاره الصبان، فإن الألوان والملابس والأجواء الحيوية تنقل جوهر الاحتفالات، التي من خلالها، يلتقط الصبان بمهارة اللحظات الهادئة، فيُجسّد النساء في محيط هادئ، أو في محادثات جانبية أو وهن منغمسات في قراءات مشتركة.

يجسد الصبان جوهر الحياة في المجتمع، وهن النساء في الأسواق المكتظة فيصورهن في الحياة العامة. وضمن هذه الأعمال تمتلئ لوحاته بنساء مجتمعات معاً حاملات السلال في الفضاء العام، وتتميَّز بالإيحاء بالبهجة والحيوية على الرغم من استخدامه للألوان الباردة مثل البنفسجي والأصفر والأخضر، ومن هذه المشاهد نتأمل دور المرأة والأعمال الشاقة الموكلة إليها اجتماعياً.

تتجلَّى في أعمال الصبان العلاقة الدقيقة بين المرأة وبيئتها سواءً الحضرية أو القروية، ويدمج العنصر النسائي بانسيابية بالمشهد المعماري باستخدام التراكيب التي تعطي إيحاءً بالسريالية؛ فتارةً يرسمها فوق المباني وتارةً يدمجها بينها، وهذا يوحي بتقدير الصبان العميق لدور المرأة في المجتمع، وغالباً ما يجمع النساء بصورٍ جماعية يدمجها مع الأسطح العمودية، وتحيط بهن مبانٍ تمثل منطقة الحجاز والمنطقة النجدية، وتارة أخرى يصور الارتباط الوثيق بين الإنسان والطبيعة، فيجمع النساء مع الغزلان والجمال والخيول وكل هذه الصور ترمز إلى العلاقة بالطبيعة وتثير الإحساس بالوحدة والتناغم معها.

life, while also reflecting on the laborious nature of women's roles in society and economy.

The intricate relationship between women and their environment, both urban and rural, unfolds in a selection of Alsabban's paintings. Women are seamlessly integrated into the architectural landscape, at times depicted atop buildings or seemingly floating amidst them, imbuing the composition with a sense of surrealism. This serves as a subtle homage to Alsabban's profound appreciation of women's role in society. Often grouped together and depicted in vertical planes, women are surrounded by buildings representative of both the Hejaz and Najd regions. Other paintings depict the symbiotic relationship between women and animals, such as deer, camels, and horses. These depictions symbolize the interplay between women and the natural world and evoke a sense of unity and connection with nature.

Alsabban's artistic perspective offers a unique portrayal of society and captures the multifaceted female influences that have shaped his worldview. In his paintings, women assume the role of custodians of tradition, embodying cultural heritage, enduring values, and timeless narratives. *Muse's Reverie* stands as a testament to the artist's dedication to honoring society and recognizing the pivotal roles played by women within it. The exhibition serves as an acknowledgment of the diverse identities and profound influences of women, while also celebrating the unwavering strength demonstrated by Saudi women throughout history and in the present.

ويقـدم المنظـور الفني للصبان صـورةً فريدة للمجتمـع؛ إذ يجسـد التأثيـر النسـائي الكبيـر عليـه وذلك ما رسـم نظرته للعالم؛ كما تأخذ النساء دور حماة التـراث في لوحاته، حيث يجسـدن الموروث الثقافـي والقيم والروايـات الخالدة.

يعتبـر معـرض «عقيلة الخيـال» بمثابة برهان علـى تفانـي الفنـان وتقديـره للمجتمـع وإقـراره بأهميـة أدوار النسـاء فيـه. وهـو اعتـراف بهويـات المـرأة المتنوعـة وتأثيرهـا العميق، واعتـزازاً بالقوة الراسـخة التي أثبتتها المرأة السعودية عبر الأجيال.

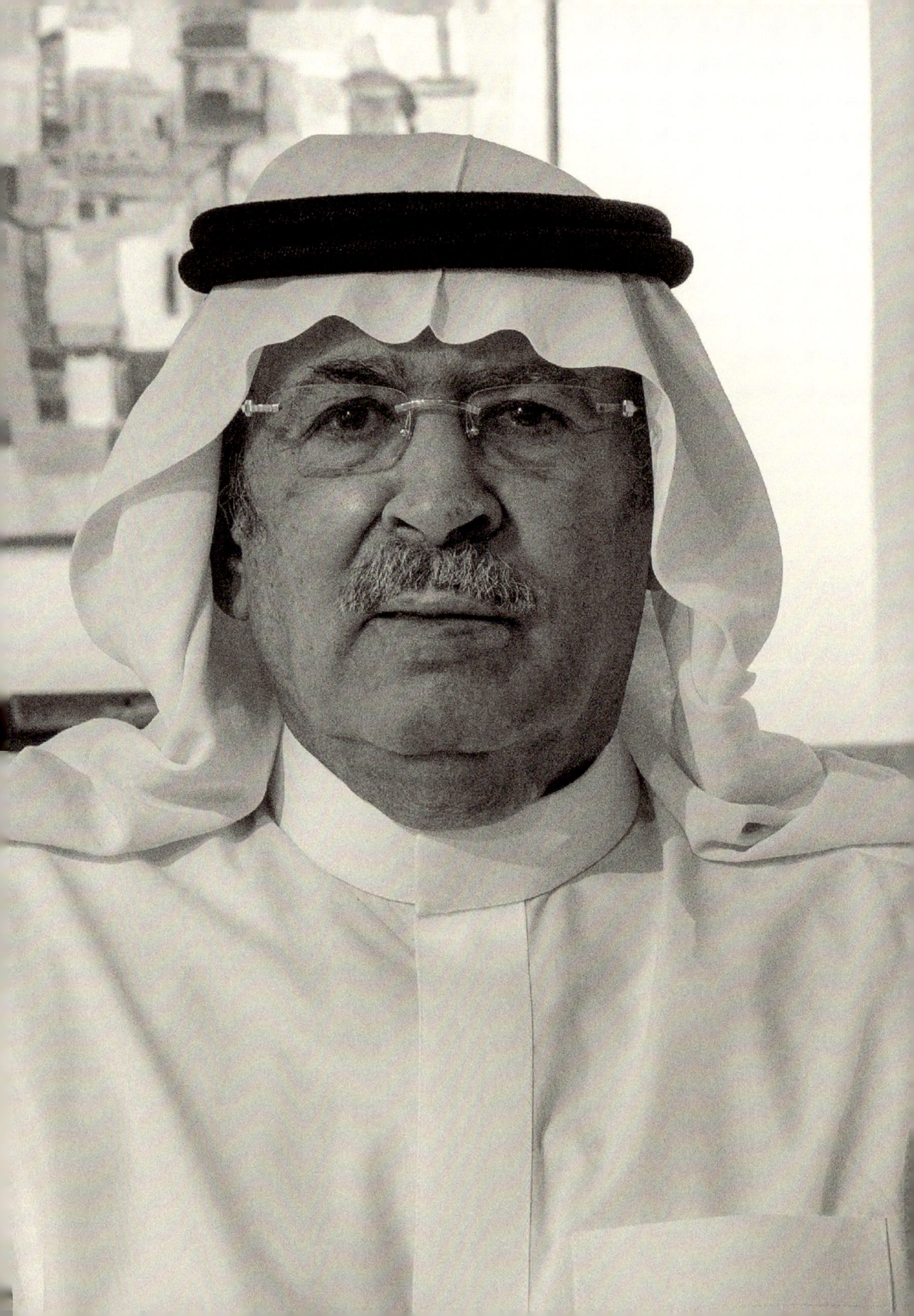

طه الصبان
Taha Alsabban

آرام العجاجي وندى العرادي
Aram Alajaji and Nada Alaradi

Painter, art practitioner, and muralist Taha Alsabban is renowned for his distinctive portrayal of elongated figures in his paintings, and exploration of subjects within the Saudi society. The self-taught painter played a significant role in fostering art communities in Jeddah. He served as the first president of the House of Artists in Jeddah, Saudi Arabia in 1993 and he has been a member of the Saudi Arabian Society of Culture and Arts since 1975, and subsequently became a board member in 2006. In addition to contributing to the art community, he held important positions within various organizations including the Television Program Director at Jeddah TV, in the Ministry of Media. Alsabban also founded and established the Taha Alsabban Construction Company.

Born in Makkah, Saudi Arabia, Alsabban received his intermediate schooling in his hometown and in Jeddah, where his interest in the arts first appeared. He initially decided to study at the Accademia di Belle Arti in Rome, Italy, in 1966, however after three months of studies, he was obliged to return to Jeddah due to his father's passing and forsake his degree. Years later, in 1975, Alsabban received a scholarship from the Ministry of Media to study in the United Kingdom. During this time, Alsabban was strongly

طه الصبان فنان عُرِف بتجسيده الشخصيات في لوحاته، واستكشافه الموضوعات الثقافية داخل المجتمع السعودي، وقد كان له دورٌ ملموس في ازدهار المجتمع الفني في جدة. عُيّن كأول رئيس لبيت التشكيليين في جدة عام 1993م، وكان عضواً في الجمعية العربية السعودية للثقافة والفنون منذ عام 1975م، وأصبح بعد ذلك عضواً في مجلس إدارتها في عام 2006م بالإضافة إلى إسهاماته في المجتمع الفني. وعمِل في مناصب مهمة في مختلف المنظمات بما في ذلك وزارة الإعلام كمخرج برامج تلفزيونية، وله كذلك شركة طه الصبان للمقاولات.

ولد طه الصبان في مكة المكرمة، وتلقى تعليمه في مسقط رأسه في مدينة جدة، حيث ظهر خلال ذلك اهتمامه بالفنون للمرة الأولى ليقرر الدراسة في أكاديمية الفنون الجميلة (أكاديميا دي بيل آرتي) في روما عام 1966م. وبعد ثلاثة أشهر من الدراسة، اضطر للعودة إلى جدة بسبب وفاة والده. بعد ذلك حصل طه الصبان على منحة دراسية من وزارة الإعلام للدراسة في المملكة المتحدة عام 1975م، وكان متحمساً آنذاك لمواصلة صقل مهاراته كرسام وكرّس الكثير من وقته الحر في الفنون.

Alsabban's experimentation also crossed into materiality. He developed a distinctive textured base for his paintings, occasionally incorporating unconventional elements such as sand and fragments of women's clothing. It was during this period that he established his most recognizable style, characterized by vibrant monochromatic color palettes portraying cityscapes and seascapes, adorned with lengthened human figures, predominantly women.

During his studies in the United Kingdom, Alsabban organized his first solo exhibitions, marking significant milestones in his artistic journey, each inaugurated by the respective mayors of the cities.

The first exhibition took place in Colchester, United Kingdom (1975); and the second was located at the Glasgow Arab Students' Club, Glasgow, Scotland (1976). As Alsabban's artistic career progressed, he continued to showcase his work through solo exhibitions in various countries. Notable among these were at the House of Artists, Jeddah, Saudi Arabia (1994); the Lebanese College of Architecture, Beirut, Lebanon (1999); and the UNESCO Palace, Beirut, Lebanon (2001). In parallel with his exhibition at the UNESCO Palace, Alsabban organized a dedicated exhibition for promising Saudi female artists, providing them with a platform to showcase their talents. During the 1990s, Alsabban also demonstrated his commitment to supporting emerging artists by establishing the *Taha Alsabban Fine Art Award for Promising Female Artists*, which financially supported female artists.

Alsabban's participation in group exhibitions began early in his artistic journey with his first group exhibition taking place at the Center for Fine Arts, Jeddah, Saudi Arabia (1967), marking his entry into the art scene. In a subsequent year, Abdulhalim Radwi organized an exhibition for graduates of Italian schools,

في المراحل الأولى مـن رحلة الصبان الفنية، درس وصقل مهاراته مـن خـلال محـاكاة الأعمال الفنيـة الكلاسـيكية، إلا أن شـغفه بالرسم بـرز بعد عودته مـن إيطاليـا؛ وكان الفنان الرائد عبـد الحليم رضـوي وصـوره لمكة مصدراً لإلهامه، حيث سـعى الصبـان للقائـه وكان لقاءً بالغ الأثر.

أدرك رضـوي إمكانيات الصبان الفنية، وأصبح فيما بعد مرشداً لـه، حيث شـجعه علـى عرض أعماله في سـن مبكرة، ما عزز من تشكيل مسـيرته الفنية. وشـهدت ممارسـته الفنية تحـولاً بتأثير من رضوي، ما دفعـه إلى المغامـرة والتجربة في عوالم فنية أخرى.

ومع اتسـاع معرفتـه الفنية وتصـوّره للقضايا الاجتماعيـة فـي الثقافة العربية مـن أعمال رضوي، اعتمد الصبان على التجريب بشكل متزايد، فامتدت مجموعتـه المتنوعة مـن الأعمال إلى حـدود فنية مختلفـة، لتتضمّن عناصر من الفن التجريدي والفن التعبيـري وأنمـاط فنيـة أخـرى، وقد أثـرت ثقافتي مكـة المكرمـة وجدة بعمـق على المـدركات الفنية للصبان، وقد وصفت أعماله بوضوح تراث المنطقة وثقافتها وعمارتها والمناظر السـاحلية والحيوانات وذلك انعكاس مباشـر للأماكن التـي عاش فيها.

وفي نهايـات القرن العشـرين تعمقت لوحاته فـي العلاقـة بيـن المدينـة وسـكانها حتـى عندمـا كان يصـوّر العمارة الحجازية بدون تجسـيد بشـري، باعتقـاده أن وجـود النـاس كان مخفيـاً بشـكل ملحـوظ، حيث إن السـرد الهـام يتشـكل من خلال تـآزر الرجـال والنسـاء وتفاعله.

كمـا وصلـت تجاربه إلى المـادة أيضاً، فقـد وضـع أساسـاً محسوسـاً مميـزاً للوحاتـه، يشـمل أحيانـاً عناصر غيـر تقليدية مثل الرمـل وقطع من ملابس نسـائية؛ وخـلال هذه الفترة رسـخ أسـلوبه الأكثر شـهرة، والذي يتميز بتشـكيلات ألوان أحادية نابضـة بالحيـاة تصوّر المناظـر الحضريـة والبحرية، مُزينـة برسـومات بشـرية ممـدودة معظمهـا مـن النسـاء فـي جميـع أعمالـه الفنية.

driven to continue honing his skills as a painter and dedicated much of his free time to the arts.

In the early stages of Alsabban's artistic journey, he studied and emulated classical artworks, honing his skills through practice. However, it was after his return from Italy that his passion for painting flourished. Inspired by the pioneering artist Abdulhalim Radwi and his portrayals of Makkah, Alsabban sought a meeting with him, resulting in an immediate and profound impact on Alsabban.

Radwi recognized Alsabban's artistic potential and subsequently became his mentor and encouraged him to exhibit work at a young age, further shaping his artistic trajectory. Alsabban's art practice transformed under Radwi's influence, prompting him to venture into experimental realms.

As Alsabban deepened his artistic knowledge and took inspiration from Radwi's exploration of social issues within Arab culture, he found himself increasingly drawn to experimental approaches in his own work. His diverse body of work traversed various stylistic boundaries, encompassing elements of abstraction, expressionism, and other artistic styles. The cultures of Makkah and Jeddah deeply influenced Alsabban's practice. His works vividly depicted the region's heritage, architecture, coastal landscapes, and animals—a direct reflection of the places he had personally experienced.

By the late twentieth century, his paintings delved further into exploring the intricate relationship between the city and its inhabitants. Even when portraying Hejazi architecture devoid of human figures, Alsabban believed that the presence of people was inherently concealed. He also believed that significant narratives are shaped through the collaboration and interaction of men and women.

أثنـاء دراسـته فـي المملكـة المتحـدة، نظـم الصبـان معارضـه الفرديـة الأولـى وافتُتـح كل منهـا بحضـور رؤسـاء البلديات، وقد أُقيـم المعرض الأول فـي كولتشيسـتر فـي المملكـة المتحـدة (1975م)؛ وكان المعـرض الثاني في نادي الطـلاب العرب في غلاسكو في أسكتلندا (1976م)، ومع تقدم مسيرته الفنيـة، اسـتمر في عرض أعماله مـن خلال معارض فردية في مختلـف البلدان، وكان من أبرزها معرضٌ فـي بيـت التشـكيليين فـي جـدة، المملكـة العربيـة السـعودية (1994م)؛ ومعرض في الكلية اللبنانية للهندسـة المعماريـة فـي بيروت، لبنـان (1999م)، وفي قصر اليونسكو فـي بيروت، لبنـان (2001م).

وبالتزامـن مـع معرضـه فـي بيـروت، نظـم معرضاً مخصصاً للفنانـات السـعوديات الواعدات مقدماً لهـن منصة لعـرض مواهبهـن الفنية خلال التسـعينيات، وقـد أظهـر التزامـه بدعـم الفنانيـن الناشئين مـن خـلال إنشـاء «جائـزة طـه الصبـان للفنـون الجميلـة للفنانـات الواعدات» وهـي جائزة تدعـم الفنانـات النسـاء مالياً.

بدأت مشـاركة الصبان في المعارض الجماعية فـي مراحـل مبكرة مـن رحلتـه الفنيـة؛ إذ أقيم أول معـرض جماعـي له فـي مركـز الفنـون الجميلة في جـدة، المملكـة العربيـة السـعودية عـام(1967م)، ليكون وسـماً لدخولـه إلـى المشـهد الفنـي. وفـي العـام التالي، نظم عبدالحليم رضوي معرضاً حصرياً لخريجـي المـدارس الإيطاليـة، وعلى الرغـم من أن الصبان تلقـى تعليمه لفترة قصيرة فـي إيطاليا، إلا أن رضوي أدرك إمكاناتـه الفنية وضمّه إلى المعرض ما أظهـر إيمانه بقـدرات الصبـان الفنية.

في عـام(1981م)، شـارك الصبـان في معرض ثلاثي بجانب الفنانين علي الغامدي وعبدالله نواوي فـي ردك بلازا في جدة، المملكة العربية السـعودية مـا أرسـى مكانته فـي المجتمـع الفنـي؛ وقـد أقام معـارض مشـتركة مـع العديـد مـن الفنانيـن مثل فـؤاد مغربـل فـي أتيلييه جـدة، المملكة العربيـة السـعودية عـام (1999م)، وعبدالله حمّـاس فـي

despite Alsabban not having graduated from Italy, Radwi recognized his artistic potential and included him in the exhibition. In 1981, Alsabban further established his presence in the art community by participating in a joint exhibition alongside artists Ali Alghamdi and Abdullah Nawawi at the Redec Plaza, Jeddah, Saudi Arabia.

Additionally, Alsabban held joint exhibitions with Dr. Fouad Mougharbel at Jeddah Altelier, Jeddah, Saudi Arabia (1999); and Abdullah Hammas at Hafez Gallery, Jeddah, Saudi Arabia (2015). Alsabban's participation in group exhibitions and biennales includes Iran Biennale, Iran (2002); International Cairo Biennale, Egypt (1994 and 1998); Sharjah Biennale, United Arab Emirates (1993 and 2001); Bank of Riyadh Exhibition, United Kingdom (1985 and 1994); Saudi Contemporary Art Exhibition, India (1984); and the Euro-Art festival, Switzerland (2000). Alsabban's artistic legacy lies in his ability to capture the essence of Saudi society, his experimentation with different styles, and his contributions to the growth of the art community. His impact on the Saudi art scene and dedication to his practice have led him to be recognized as a prominent figure in Saudi art history.

حافظ جاليري في جدة، المملكة العربية السعودية عـام (2015م)، ويتضمن سـجل مشـاركات الصبان معـارض وبينـاليـات بـارزة حـول العالـم، بمـا فـي ذلـك بينالـي إيـران (2002م)؛ وبينالـي القاهـرة الدولي (1994 و1998م)؛ وبينالي الشارقة (1993 و2001م)؛ ومعـرض بنـك الريـاض في المملكـة المتحـدة (1985م)؛ ومعـرض الفـن السـعودي المعاصر في الهند (1984م)؛ بالإضافة إلى مهرجان الفن الأوروبي في سويسرا (2000م). ويتمثل الإرث الفنـي لطـه الصبان فـي قدرتـه على تصويـر جوهر المجتمـع السـعودي وتجاربه فـي مختلف الأنماط الفنيـة، وقـد أدى تأثيـره علـى المشـهد الفنـي في المملكـة وتفانيـه فـي ممارسـاته الفنيـة إلـى تميزه كشـخصية بـارزة في تاريـخ الفن السـعودي.

التسلســـل الزمني لسيرة الفنــان
Artist Timeline

Taha Alsabban was born in Makkah, Saudi Arabia	**1948**	وُلد طه الصبان في مكة المكرمة بالمملكة العربية السعودية
Art was incorporated into the general education curriculum across Saudi Arabia	**1958**	دمج الفن في المناهج الدراسية لجميع المستويات في المدارس الحكومية في نظام التعليم العام في المملكة العربية السعودية
Alsabban moved to Italy to study arts and returned to Jeddah, Saudi Arabia after three months	**1966**	ســافر الصبان إلى إيطاليا لدراسة الفنون وعاد بعد 3 أشـهر إلى جدة، المملكة العربية السعودية
Alsabban began working with Jeddah TV and later became a television program director at the Ministry of Media until 1978	**1967**	بــدأ العمـل فـي تلفزيـون جـدة، ثـم أصبـح مديـراً للبرامج التلفزيونيـة فـي وزارة الإعـلام حتـى 1978م
The Center for Fine Arts was established by the Ministry of Education and managed by Abdulhalim Radwi in Jeddah, Saudi Arabia		أسست وزارة التعليم مركز الفنون الجميلة بجدة في المملكة العربية السعودية، تحت إدارة الفنان عبدالحليم رضوي
Alsabban participated in the first group exhibition at The Center for Fine Arts in Jeddah, Saudi Arabia		شــارك الصبان في معرض جماعي في مركز الفنون الجميلة بجدة، المملكة العربية السعودية
Alsabban participated in the Saudi-Italian group exhibition at The Center for Fine Arts in Jeddah, Saudi Arabia	**1972**	شــارك في المعــرض السـعودي الإيطالي الجماعـي في مركز الفنـون الجميلة بجدة، المملكة العربية الســعودية
The Saudi Arabian Society for Culture and Arts was established in Riyadh, Saudi Arabia, which opened thirteen branches in the following years across Saudi Arabia, beginning with Jeddah in 1974	**1973**	تأسســت الجمعيـة العربيـة السـعودية للثقافة والفنون في الريـاض، والتـي افتتحـت فـي السـنوات التاليـة 13 فرعاً في جميع أنحـاء المملكة بدايةً بمدينة جدة في عـام 1974م
The General Presidency of Youth Welfare was established as an independent governmental institution with a dedicated department for fine arts	**1974**	تأسســت الرئاسـة العامة لرعايـة الشـباب كجهـة حكوميـة مسـتقلة تضـم قسـماً متخصصاً فـي الفنـون الجميلـة
Alsabban was awarded a scholarship to study in the United Kingdom from the Ministry of Media	**1975**	حصـل علـى منحـة مـن وزارة الإعلام للدراسـة فـي بريطانيا حتـى 1976م
Alsabban held his first solo exhibition in London, United Kingdom		افتتح المعرض الفردي الأول في كولشيستر في المملكة المتحدة
Alsabban became a member of the Saudi Arabian Society for Culture and Arts		أصبـح الصبـان عضـواً فـي الجمعيـة العربيـة السـعودية للثقافة والفنون
Alsabban held his second solo exhibition at the Glasgow Arab Students' Club in Scotland, United Kingdom	**1976**	افتتـح المعرض الفـردي الثاني في نادي الطـلاب العرب في غلاسـكو في اسكتلندا
Alsabban won the General Exhibition Award for the Kingdom's Regions organized by The General Presidency for Youth Welfare	**1980**	فاز الصبان بجائزة المعرض العام لمناطـق المملكة الـذي نظمته الرئاسـة العامة لرعاية الشـباب
Alsabban participated in a joint exhibition with Ali Alghamdi and Abdullah Nawawi at Redec Plaza, in Jeddah, Saudi Arabia	**1981**	أقـام الصبـان معرضاً مشـتركاً مـع علـي الغامـدي وعبدالله نـواوي فـي ردك بـلازا بجـدة، المملكـة العربية السـعودية
Alsabban participated in Saudi Art Cultural Week in India, organized by The General Presidency of Youth Welfare	**1984**	شارك في الأسبوع الثقافي الفني السعودي في الهند، والذي نظمته الرئاسة العامة لرعاية الشباب
Abdul Raouf Khalil Museum was established in Jeddah, Saudi Arabia, which later acquired Alsabban's artworks	**1985**	أُنشئ متحف عبدالـرؤوف خليل في جدة، المملكة العربية السعودية والذي اقتنى فيما بعد أعمال طه الصبان الفنية
Alsabban participated in the Riyadh Bank group exhibition in London, United Kingdom, organized by the Saudi Arabian Society for Culture and Arts		شارك الصبان فـي معرض جماعـي فـي لنـدن، المملكـة المتحـدة، والـذي كان لبنـك الريـاض ومن تنظيـم الجمعية العربيـة السـعودية للثقافـة والفنون

1989

Al-Muftaha Arts Village was founded in Abha, Saudi Arabia, by the Governor of Asir Prince Khalid bin Faisal AlSaud

تأسســت قريــة المفتاحــة على يــد أمير منطقــة عـسير الأمير خالــد بــن فيصــل آل سـعود

1991

Alsabban was appointed as the head of the Fine Arts Department at the Saudi Society for Culture and Arts in Jeddah, Saudi Arabia

أصبح الصبان رئيساً لقسم الفنون التشكيلية فـي الجمعية السعودية للثقافة والفنون بجدة، المملكة العربية السعودية

1992

Alsabban won the second prize in the first Malwan Art Competition by the Saudi Arabian Airlines and the second prize in the two subsequent competitions

حصل على جائزة المركز الثاني في النسخة الأولى لمسابقة مَلون السعودية التي نظمتها الخطـوط الجوية السـعودية، وفاز كـذلك بالمركز الثاني في النسختين التاليتين

1993

Alsabban was appointed as the first president of the House of Artists in Jeddah, Saudi Arabia

أصبـح الصبـان أول رئيـس لبيـت التشكـيليين فـي جـدة، المملكة العربية السعودية

Alsabban participated in the first Sharjah Biennale, Sharjah, United Arab Emirates

شــارك فــي بينالـي الشـارقة فـي الشـارقة، دولة الإمـارات العربية المتحدة

Alsabban held a solo exhibition *Taha Alsabban: Colorful Memories* at the House of Artists in Jeddah, Saudi Arabia

أقام المعرض الفردي بعنوان طه الصبان، ذكريات ملونة في بيت التشكيليين بجدة، المملكة العربية السعودية

1994

Alsabban participated in the *International Cairo Biennale*, Cairo, Egypt and once again in 1998

شـارك في بينالي القاهـرة الدولي في القاهرة، مصر وكانـت لـه مشاركة أخرى في عام 1998م

1996

Jeddah Atelier was established in Jeddah, Saudi Arabia

أُنشئت مؤسسة أتيلييه جدة، المملكة العربية السعودية

Alsabban participated in *The Four* a joint exhibition with Naiel Mulla, Abdulrahman Alsoliman, and Abdulla Alsheikh at Jeddah Atelier, Jeddah, Saudi Arabia

شارك الصبان في معرض مشترك بعنوان الأربعة مع نايل مـلا وعبدالرحمن سليمان وعبدالله الشـيخ في أتيلييه جدة، المملكة العربية السعودية

Alsabban held a joint exhibition with Farouk Kondakji in Jeddah, Saudi Arabia

أقـام المعرض الثنائي مع الفنان فـاروق القندقجي بجدة، المملكة العربية السـعودية

Alsabban participated in the 12th *Kuwait International Biennale*, organized by the Kuwait Society of Formative Arts, in Kuwait City

شـارك في بينالي الكويـت الدولي الثاني عشر والذي نظمته الجمعية الكويتية للفنون التشكيلية

1997

Alsabban held his fourth solo exhibition at the Saudi-German Hospital to support the Cancer Patients Network in Jeddah, Saudi Arabia

أقام معرضاً فردياً في المستشفى السعودي الألماني بجدة، المملكة السـعودية العربية لدعم المصابين بمرض السـرطان

1998

Alsabban participated in *Selections from Saudi Plastic Arts* touring exhibition at the Cairo Opera House, Egypt (1998); Islamic Cultural Hall, Madrid, Spain (1999); San Yang Center, Taiwan (2000); and London, United Kingdom (2000)

أُقيم المعرض المتجول مختارات من الفن التشكيلي السعودي الذي افتتح في دار الأوبرا المصرية، ثم انتقل إلى قاعة الثقافية الإسلامية بمدريد بإسبانيا (1999م)؛ ثم مركز سان يانغ، تايبيه، تايوان (2000م)؛ ثم لندن، المملكة المتحدة (2000م)

1999

Alsabban held a solo exhibition at the Saudi Arabian Society of Arts and Culture in Madinah, Saudi Arabia

أقـام معرضاً فردياً في الجمعيـة العربية السعوديـة للثقافة والفنــون بالمدينة المنورة، المملكـة العربية السعودية

Alsabban held a solo exhibition in Sharjah, United Arab Emirates, organized by The General Presidency of Youth Welfare

أقـام معرضـاً فردياً فـي الشارقـة بدولة الإمـارات العربيـة المتحـدة مـن تنظيـم الرئاسـة العامـة لرعاية الشـباب

Alsabban held a solo exhibition at the Lebanese College of Architecture in Beirut, Lebanon, and organized an exhibition for promising Saudi female artists

أقـام معرضـاً فردياً فـي بيـروت بكليـة الهندسـة المعمارية اللبنانية،ونظم معرضـاً للفنانـات السـعوديات الواعـدات

Alsabban held a solo exhibition in Sidon, Lebanon

أقام معرضاً فردياً في صيدا، لبنان

Alsabban participated in the 14th AlJanadriyah Heritage Festival and won first place

شــارك فـي مهرجـان الجنادريـة التراثـي الرابع عشر وحصل علـى جائزة المركـز الأول

Alsabban received Al-Muftaha Award in Asir, Saudi Arabia

حصل على جائزة المفتاحة في عسير، المملكة العربية السعودية

Alsabban participated in a joint exhibition with Dr. Fouad Mougharbel at Jeddah Atelier, Jeddah Saudi Arabia

أقام الصبان معرضاً مشـتركاً مع الفنان د.فـؤاد المغربل في أتيلييه جدة، في المملكة العربية السـعودية

Alsabban participated in *East and West,* a joint exhibition with Abdullah Hammas, Abdullah Alsheikh, and Abdulrahman Alsoliman in Dharan, Saudi Arabia

شـارك في معرض جماعي بعنوان شـرق وغرب مع عبدالله حمـاس وعبدالله الشـيخ وعبدالرحمن سـليمان في الظهران

Alsabban pubished his first book *Features of a Journey*	**2001**	أصدر كتاباً بعنوان ملامح من المشوار
Alsabban held a solo exhibition at the UNESCO Palace in Beirut, Lebanon		أقام معرضاً فردياً في قصر الأونيسكو في بيروت، لبنان
Alsabban held a solo exhibition at Khan El Franj in Sidon, Lebanon	**2002**	أقام معرضاً فردياً في خان الإفرنج في صيدا، لبنان
Alsabban held a solo exhibition at the Cairo Opera House in Cairo, Egypt		أقام معرضاً فردياً في دار الأوبرا المصرية بالقاهرة، مصر
Alsabban participated in the 18th Janadriyah Exhibition under the National Heritage and Culture Festival organized by the Ministry of National Guard	**2003**	شارك في معرض الجنادرية الثامن عشر الذي نظمته وزارة الحرس الوطني
Alsabban won first prize at *The Contemporary Saudi Art Exhibition*, Riyadh, Saudi Arabia	**2006**	حصل على الجائزة الأولى في معرض الفن السعودي المعاصر بالرياض، المملكة العربية السعودية
Alsabban joined the board of directors of the Saudi Arabian Society for Culture and Arts		انضم إلى مجلس إدارة الجمعية العربية السعودية للثقافة والفنون
Alsabban held a solo exhibition at Atelier Jeddah, Saudi Arabia	**2007**	أقام معرضاً فردياً في أتيلييه جدة، المملكة العربية السعودية
Alsabban's second book *Art of Taha Al-Sabban* was published by Dar Nelson, Lebanon		صدر الكتاب الثاني لطه الصبان "فن طه الصبان" نشر دار نيلسون، لبنان
Alsabban held a solo exhibition at Al Khozama Art Gallery in Riyadh, Saudi Arabia	**2008**	أقام معرضاً فردياً في الخزامى آرت جاليري بالرياض، المملكة العربية السعودية
Alsabban held a solo exhibition at Atelier Jeddah, Saudi Arabia, in support of the Wedad Charity Association	**2009**	أقام معرضاً فردياً بأتيلييه جدة، المملكة العربية السعودية، دعماً لجمعية الوداد الخيرية
Alsabban held a solo exhibition titled *Taha Alsabban in the Sixties*, at Jeddah Atelier, Saudi Arabia	**2011**	أقام معرضاً شخصياً في اتيلييه جدة، المملكة العربية السعودية، بعنوان ستينيات طه الصبان
Alsabban participated in *AlTaliaa: The Beginnings of Fine Art in Saudi Arabia* group exhibition at Ayyam Gallery in Jeddah, Saudi Arabia	**2014**	شارك في المعرض الجماعي الطليعة: بدايات الفنون الجميلة في المملكة العربية السعودية في معرض أيام غاليري في جدة
Hafez gallery was founded in Jeddah, Saudi Arabia		تأسس حافظ جاليري في جدة، المملكة العربية السعودية
Nesma Art Gallery was founded in Jeddah, Saudi Arabia		تأسس جاليري نسما آرت في جدة، المملكة العربية السعودية
Sotheby's auctioned Alsabban's painting *The House of Artists* (1993)		بيعت لوحة للصبان بعنوان بيت التشكيليين 1993م في مزاد سوثبي
Alsabban participated in a joint exhibition with Abdullah Hamas at Hafez Gallery in Jeddah, Saudi Arabia	**2015**	أقام الصبان معرضاً مشتركاً مع عبدالله حماس في حافظ جاليري جدة، المملكة العربية السعودية
Misk Art Institute was established in Riyadh, Saudi Arabia	**2017**	تأسس معهد مسك للفنون في الرياض، المملكة العربية السعودية
Mono Gallery was founded in Riyadh, Saudi Arabia		تأسيس مونو جاليري في الرياض، المملكة العربية السعودية
Alsabban held a solo exhibition at Nesma Gallery titled *Person and Place* in Riyadh, Saudi Arabia		أقام معرضاً فردياً بعنوان الإنسان والمكان بجاليري نسما في الرياض، المملكة العربية السعودية
Alsabban participated in *Decades* exhibition at Mono Gallery, Riyadh, Saudi Arabia	**2018**	شارك في معرض عقود في مونو جاليري في الرياض، المملكة العربية السعودية
Alsabban held a solo exhibition titled *Wejdan* at Mono Gallery, Riyadh, Saudi Arabia		أقام معرضاً فردياً بعنوان وجدان بمونو جاليري في الرياض، المملكة العربية السعودية
Alsabban was honored by Misk Art Institute as a pioneer in the Saudi Arts		حصل طه الصبان على جائزة كأحد روّاد الفن في المملكة العربية السعودية من معهد مسك للفنون
Alsabban participated in *Echoing the Land* group exhibition featuring pioneering artists in Saudi Arabia, by Misk Art Institute, in Riyadh, Saudi Arabia	**2023**	شارك الصبان في معرض من حولهم لمجموعة من رواد الفن السعودي، من تنظيم معهد مسك للفنون في الرياض، المملكة العربية السعودية

الأعمال الفنية

Artworks

Moonlight, 1975

Oil on canvas
60 × 46 cm
Courtesy of the artist

شعاع القمر، 1975

ألوان زيتية على قماش
60 × 46 سم
بإذن من الفنان

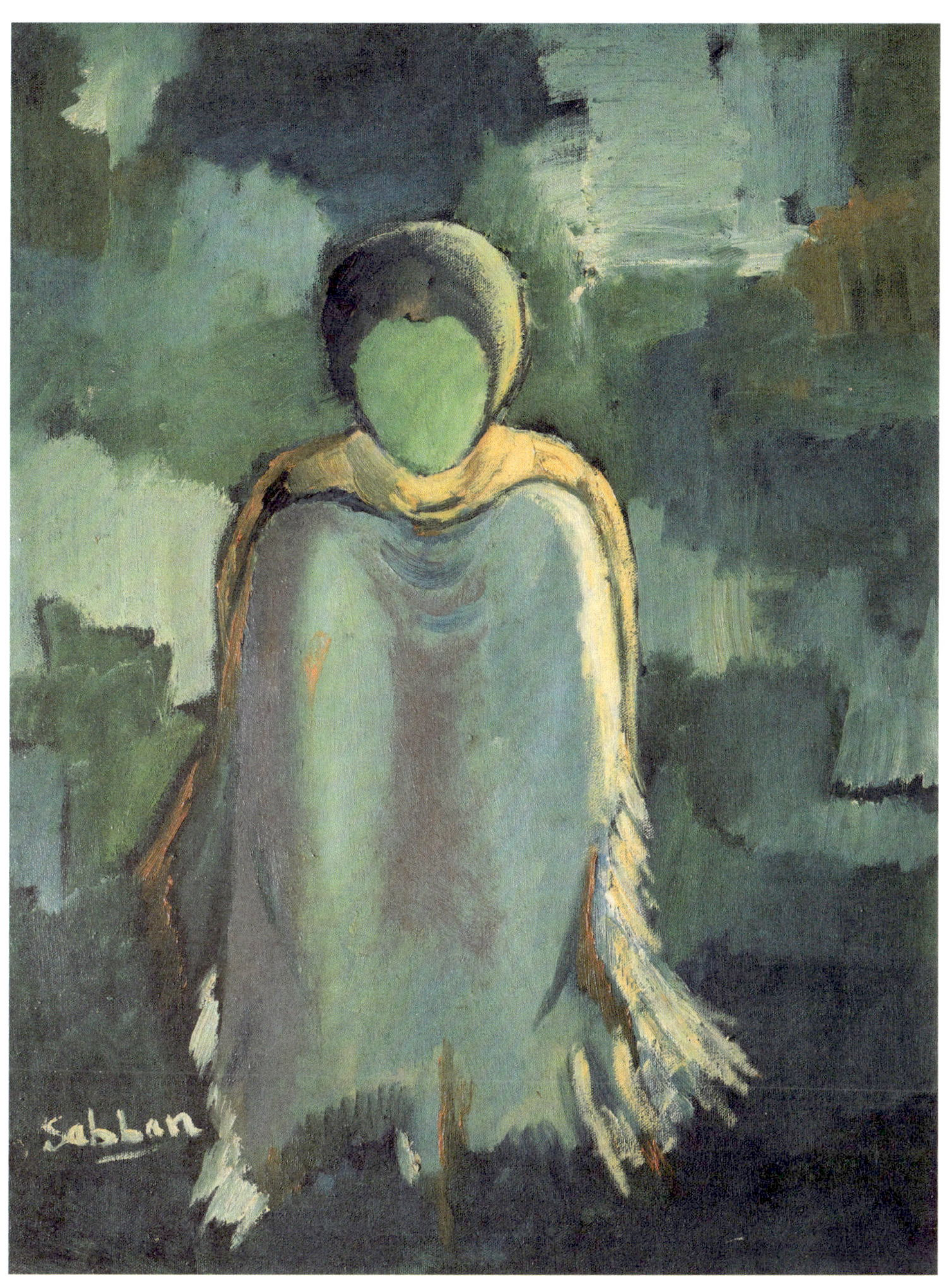

Sabban

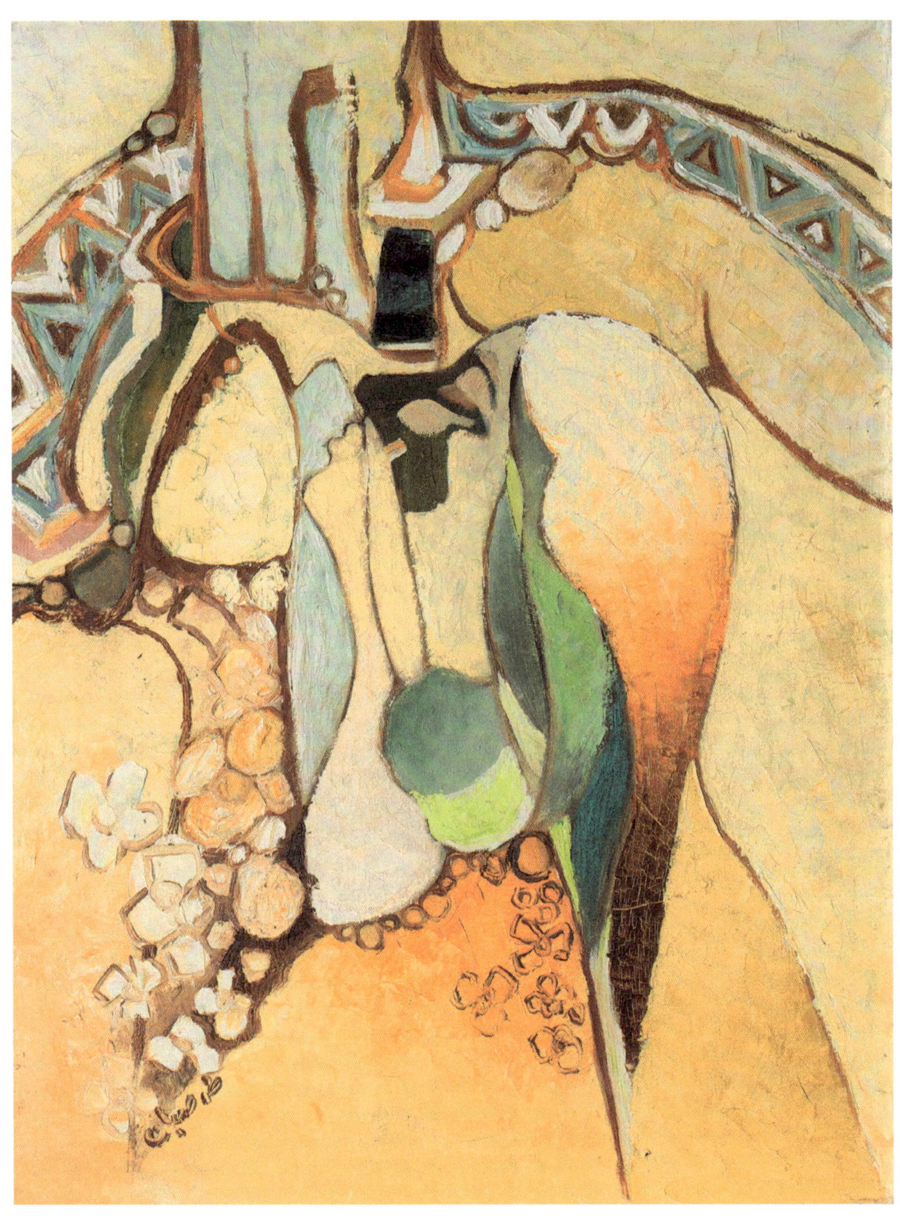

بدون عنوان، 1976

ألوان زيتية على قماش
61 × 45 سم
بإذن من الفنان

Untitled, 1976

Oil on canvas
61 × 45 cm
Courtesy of the artist

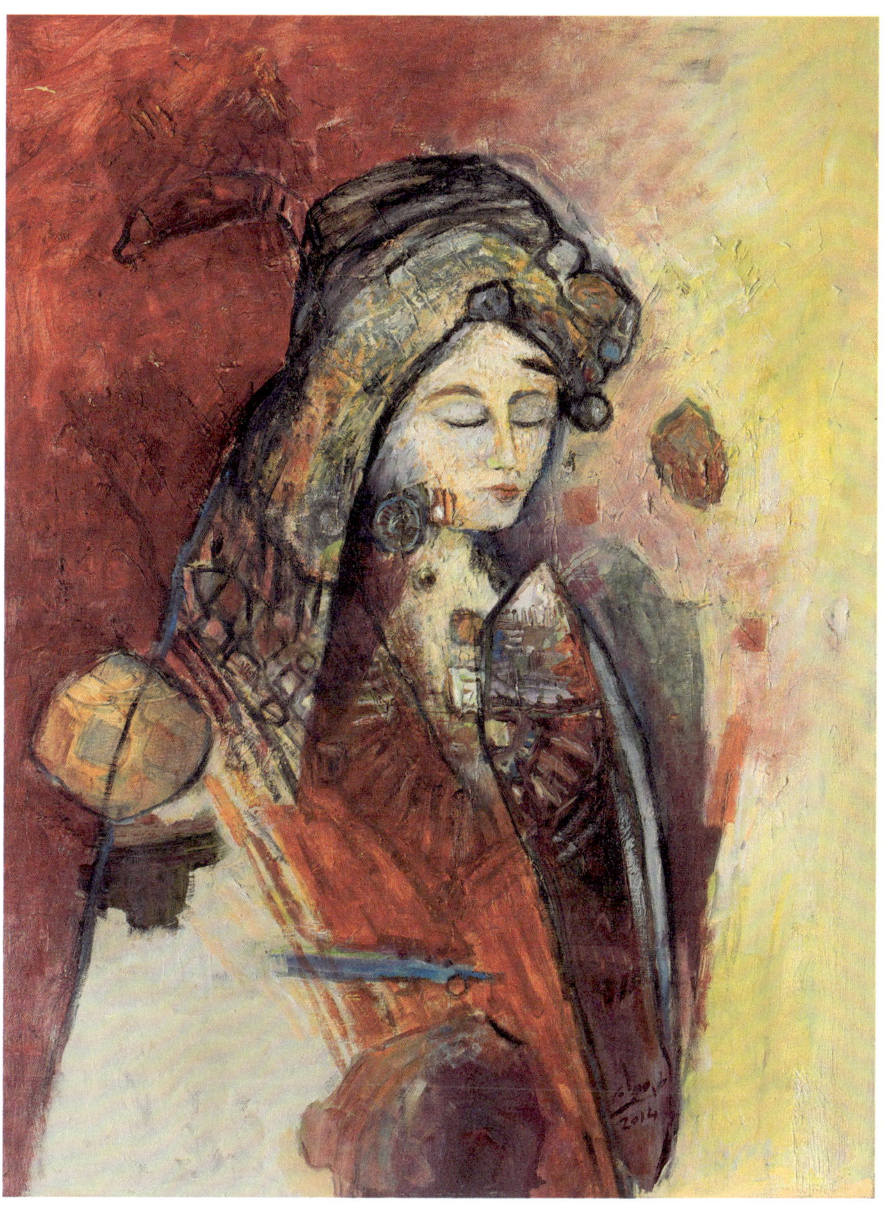

إمرأة عربية، 2014

ألوان زيتية على قماش
76 × 56 سم
بإذن من الفنان

Arab Woman, 2014

Oil on canvas
76 × 56 cm
Courtesy of the artist

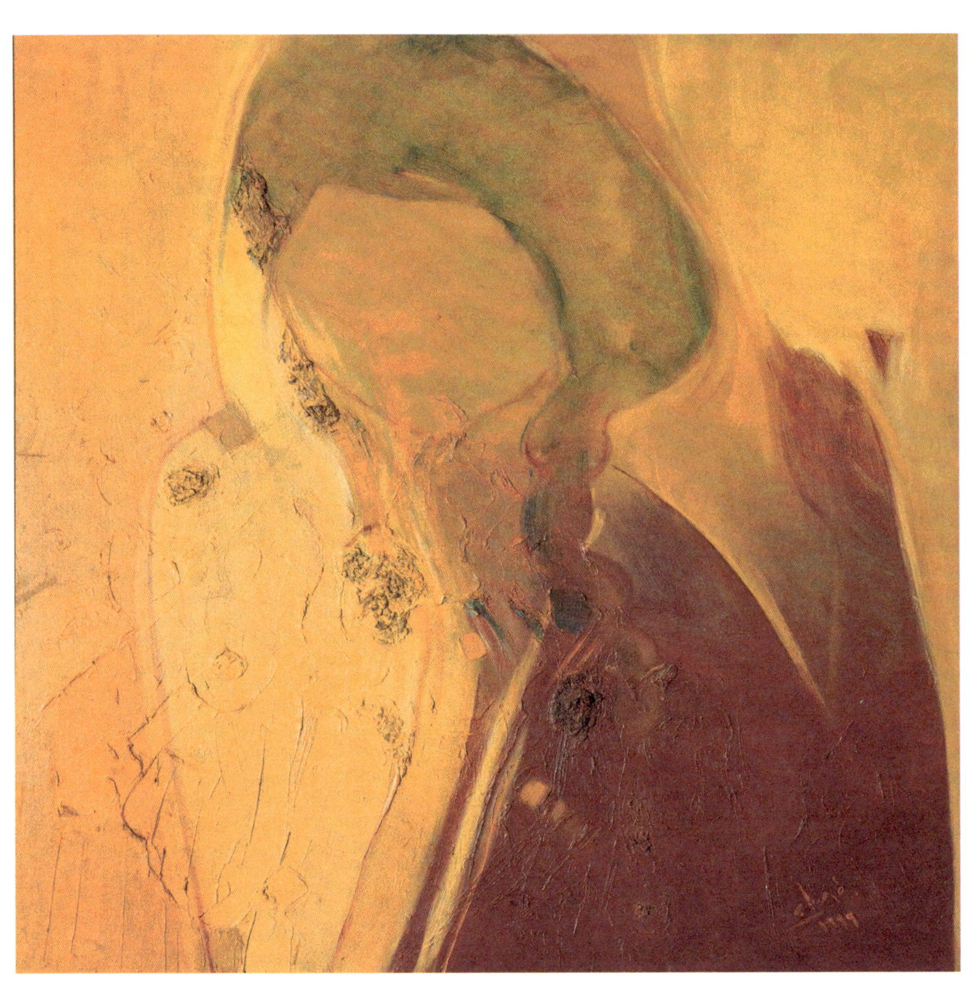

Woman, 1999

Oil on canvas
80 × 80 cm
Courtesy of the artist

إمرأة، 1999

ألوان زيتية على قماش
80 × 80 سم
بإذن من الفنان

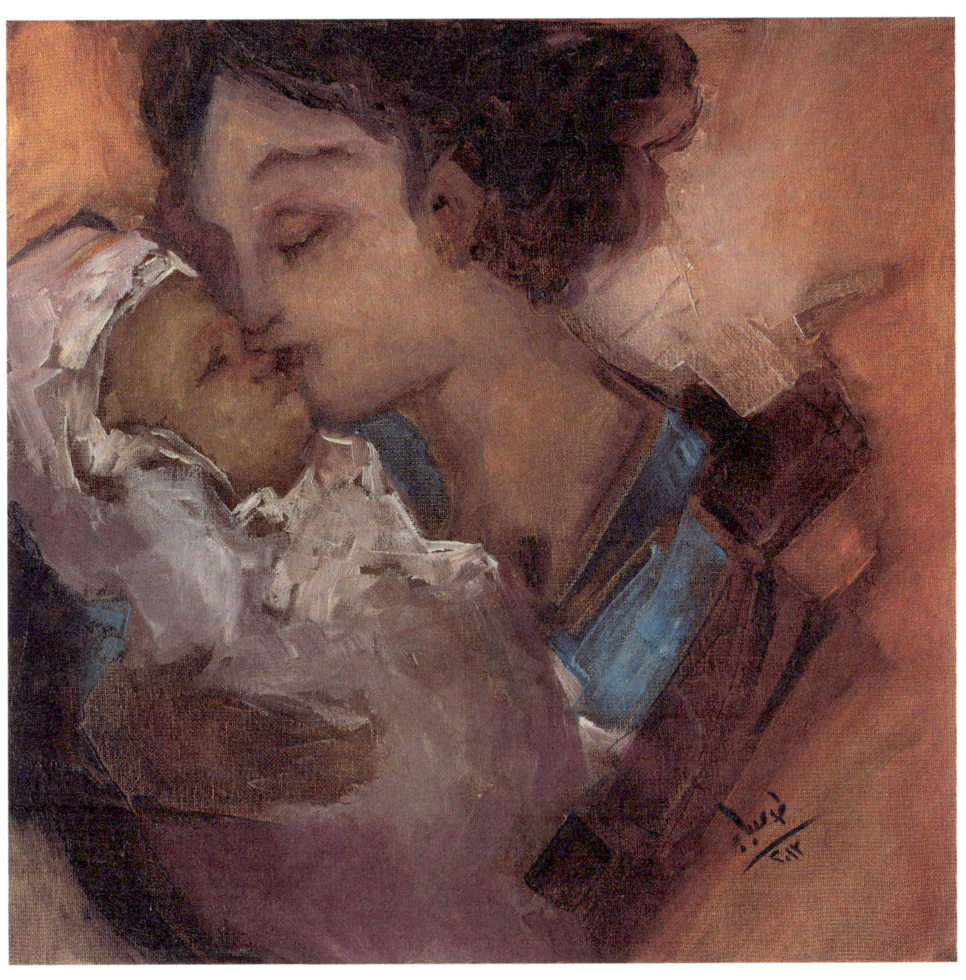

ألوان زيتية على قماش
40 × 40 سم
بإذن من الفنان

Oil on canvas
40 × 40 cm
Courtesy of the artist

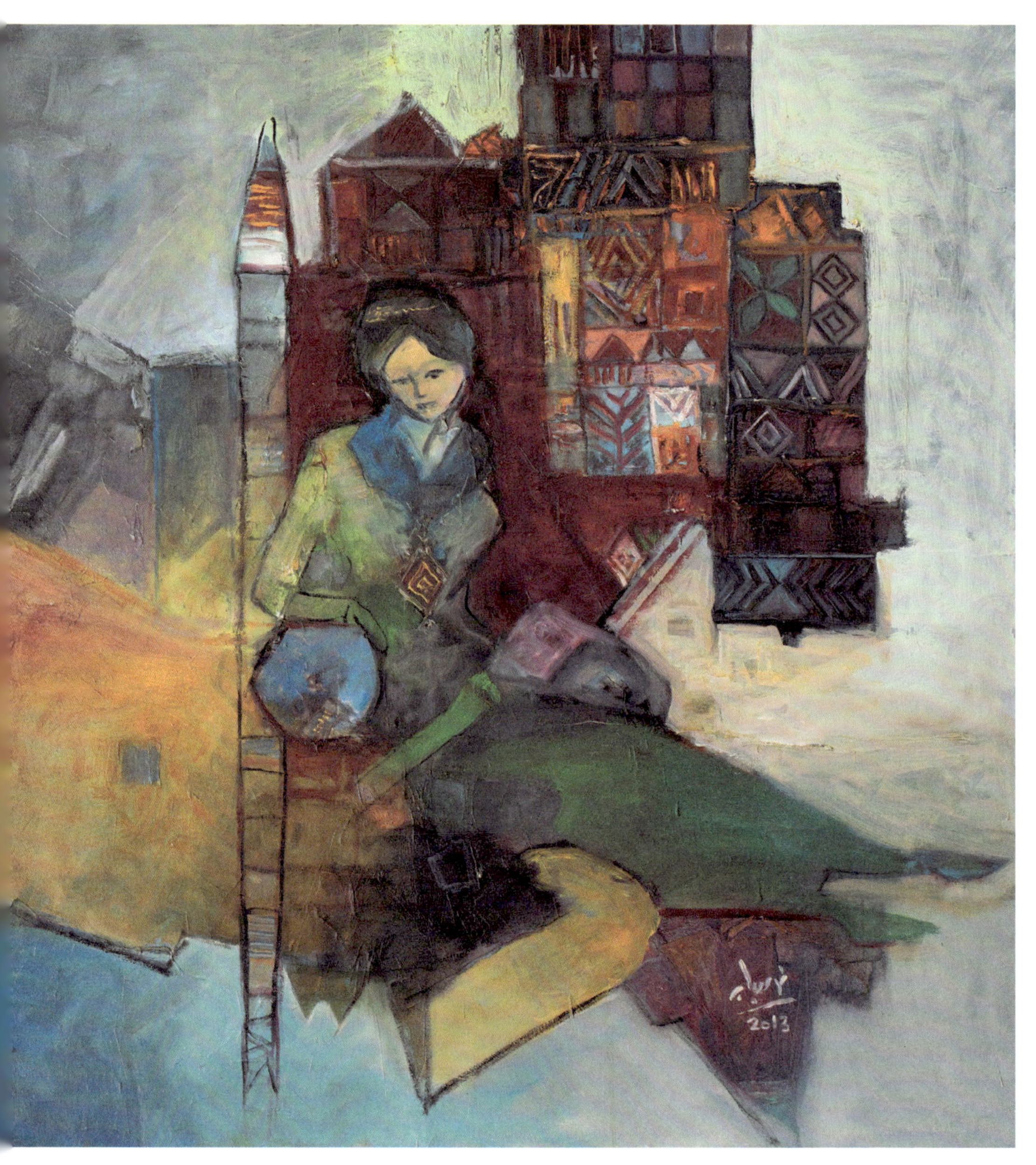

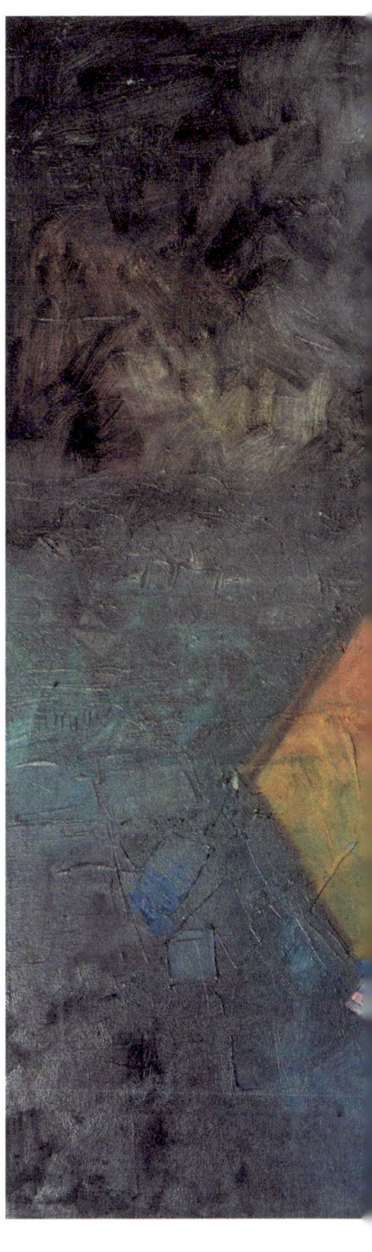

Untitled, 2013

Oil on canvas
70 × 100 cm
Courtesy of the artist

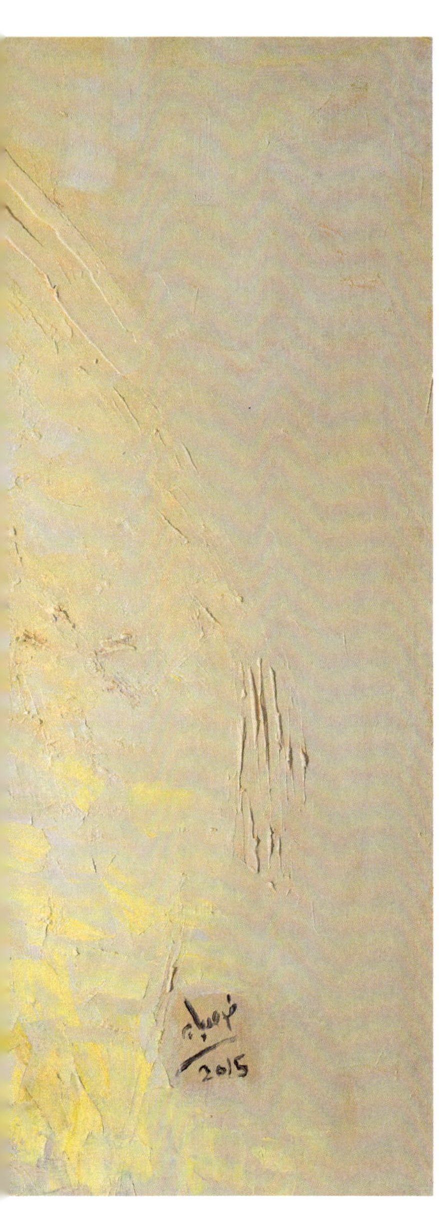

إمرأة، 2015

ألوان زيتية على قماش
76 × 101 سم
بإذن من الفنان

Woman, 2015

Oil on canvas
76 × 101 cm
Courtesy of the artist

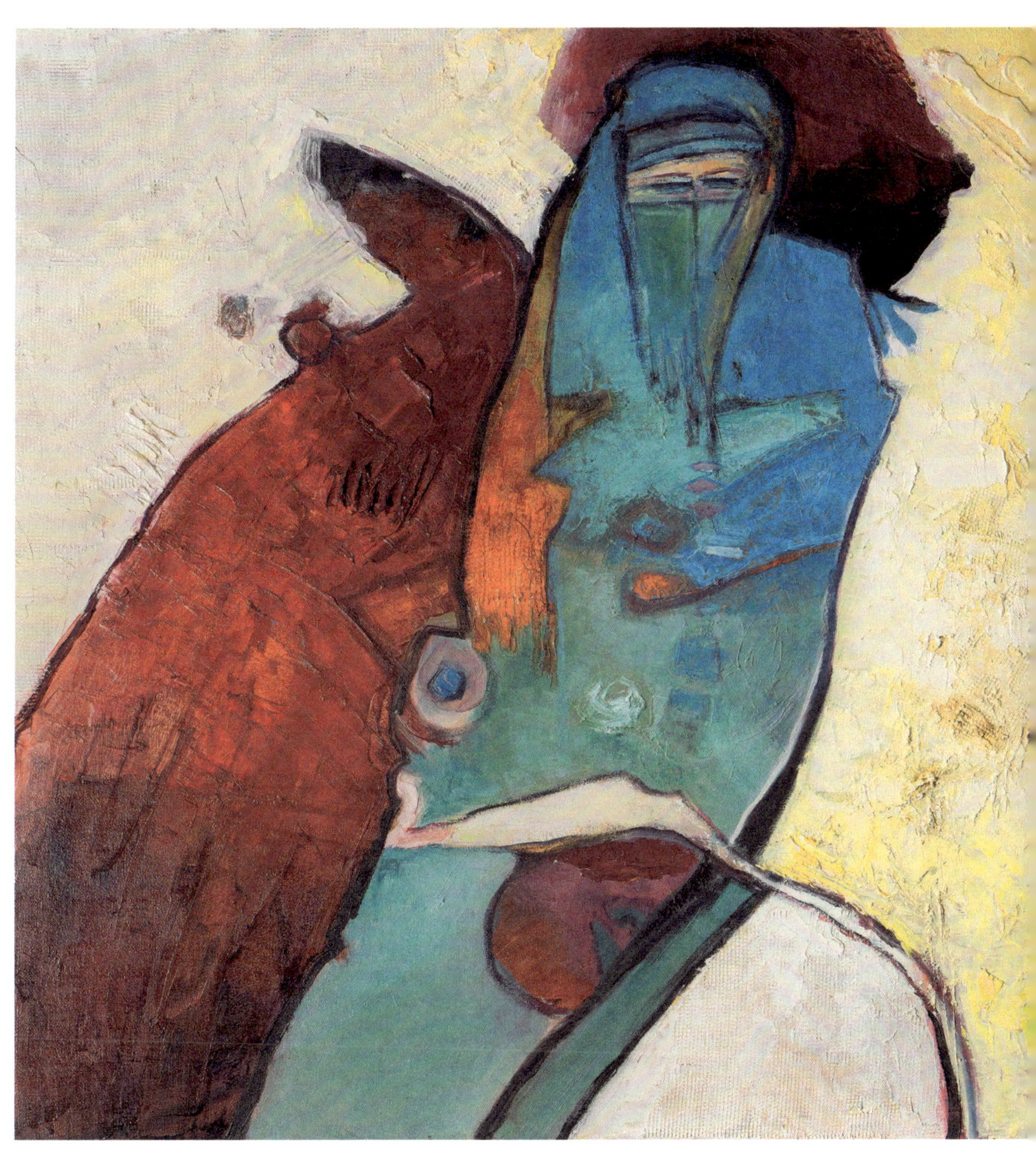

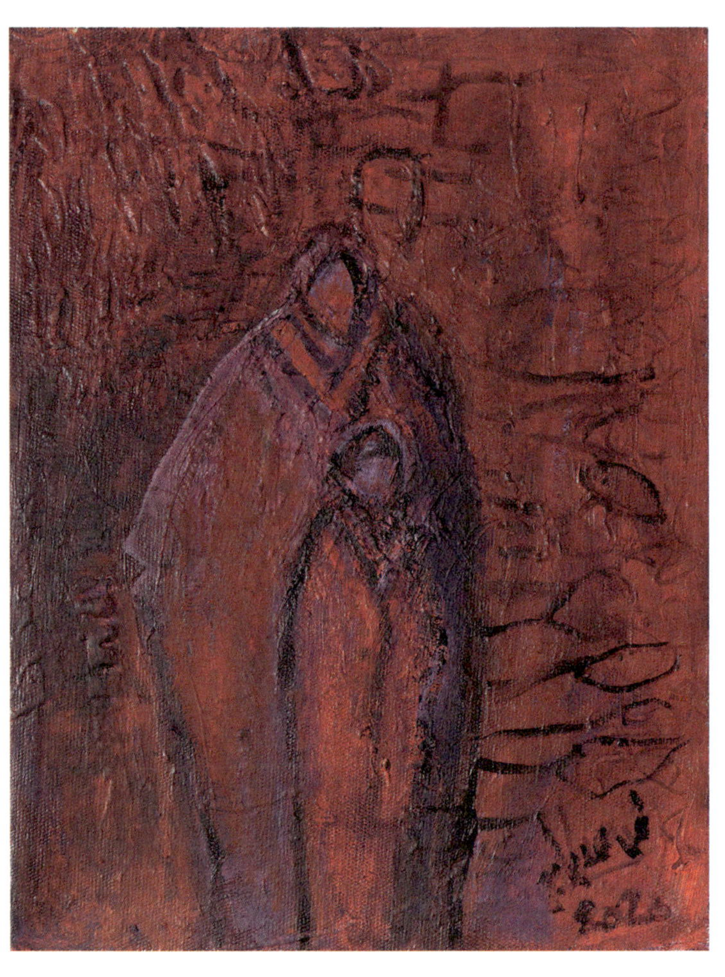

Untitled, 2020

Oil on canvas
40 × 30 cm
Courtesy of the artist

بدون عنوان، 2020

ألوان زيتية على قماش
40 × 30 سم
بإذن من الفنان

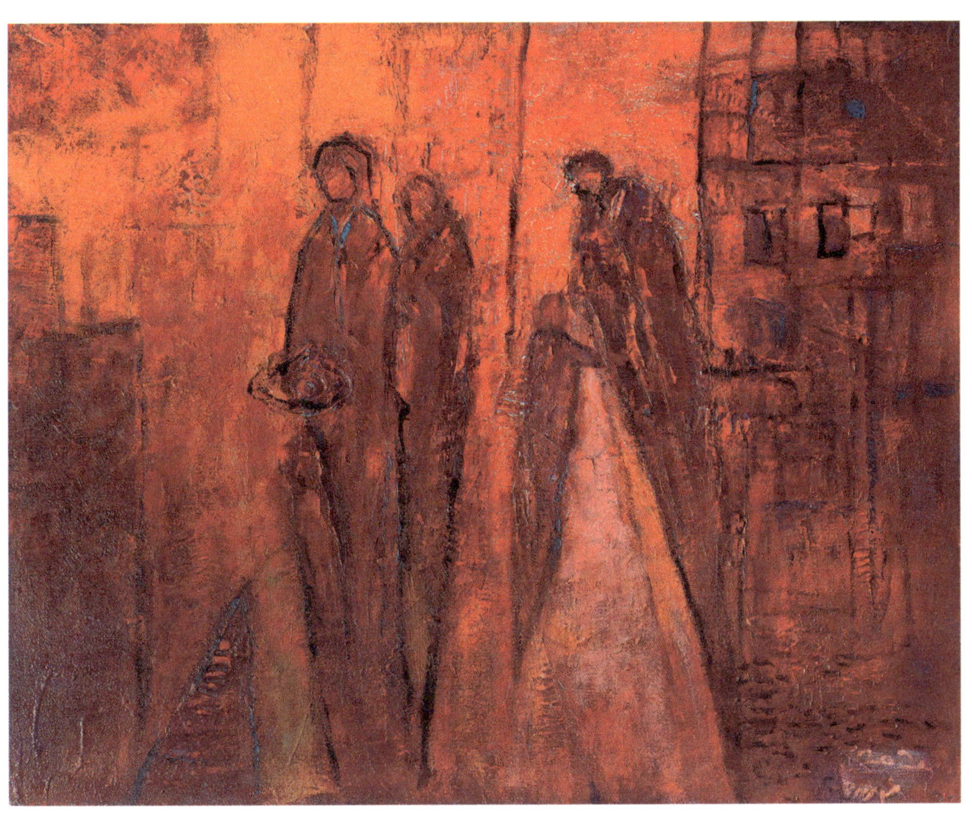

بدون عنوان، 2020

ألوان زيتية على قماش
63 × 76 سم
بإذن من الفنان

Untitled, 2020

Oil on canvas
63 × 76 cm
Courtesy of the artist

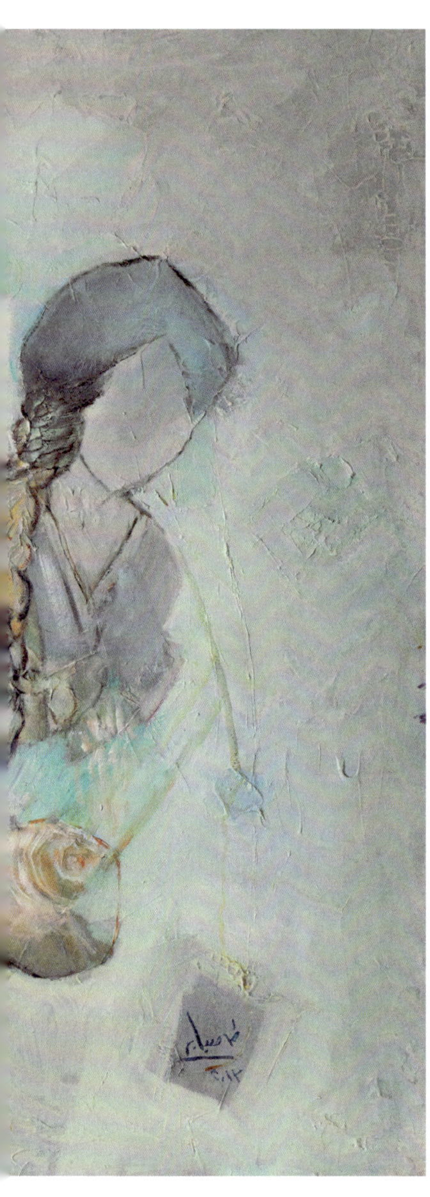

بدون عنوان، 2013

ألوان زيتية على قماش
91 × 122 سم
بإذن من الفنان

Untitled, 2013

Oil on canvas
91 × 122 cm
Courtesy of the artist

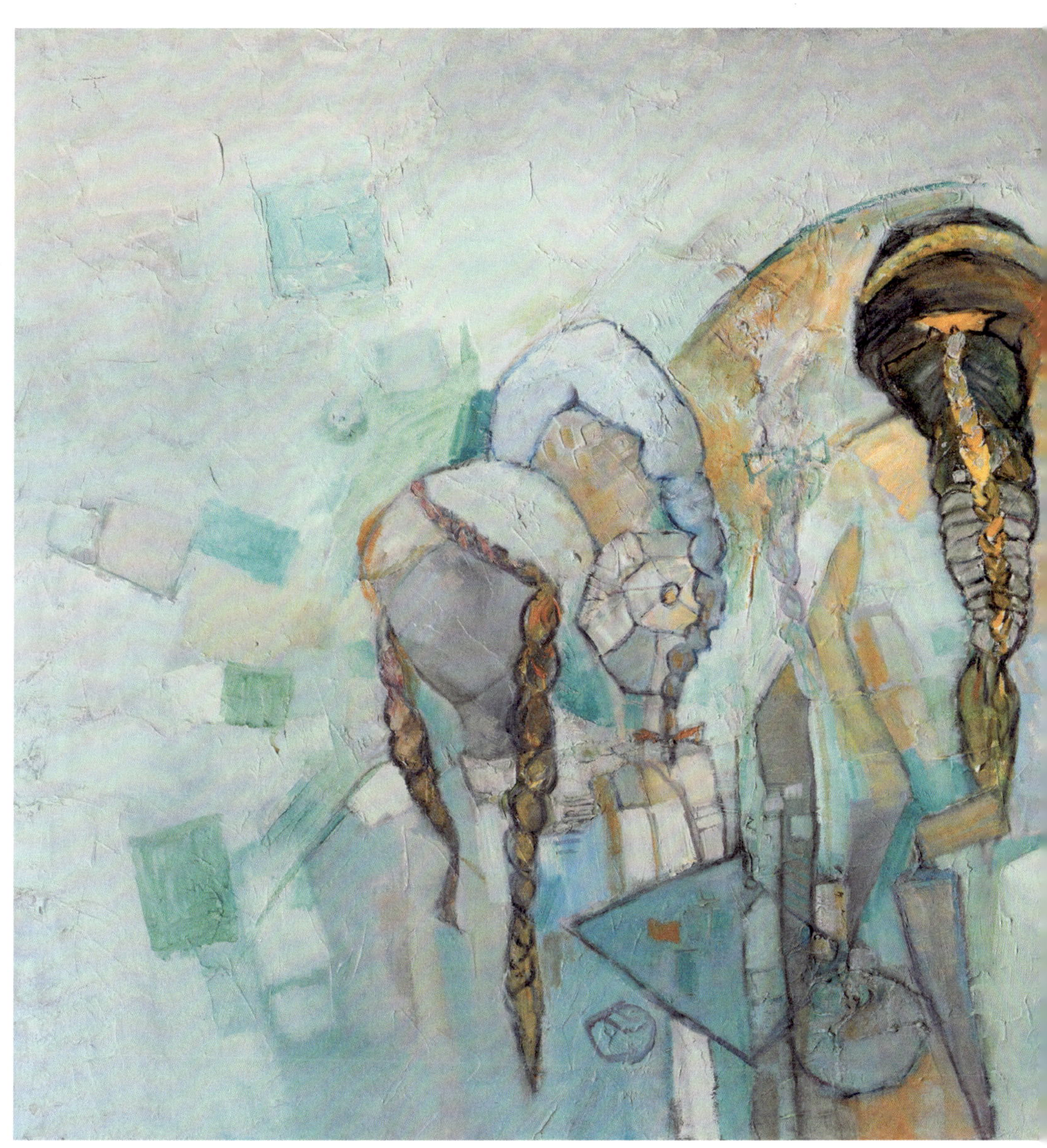

Untitled, 2020

Oil on canvas
50 × 60 cm
Courtesy of the artist

بدون عنوان، 2020

ألوان زيتية على قماش
50 × 60 سم
بإذن من الفنان

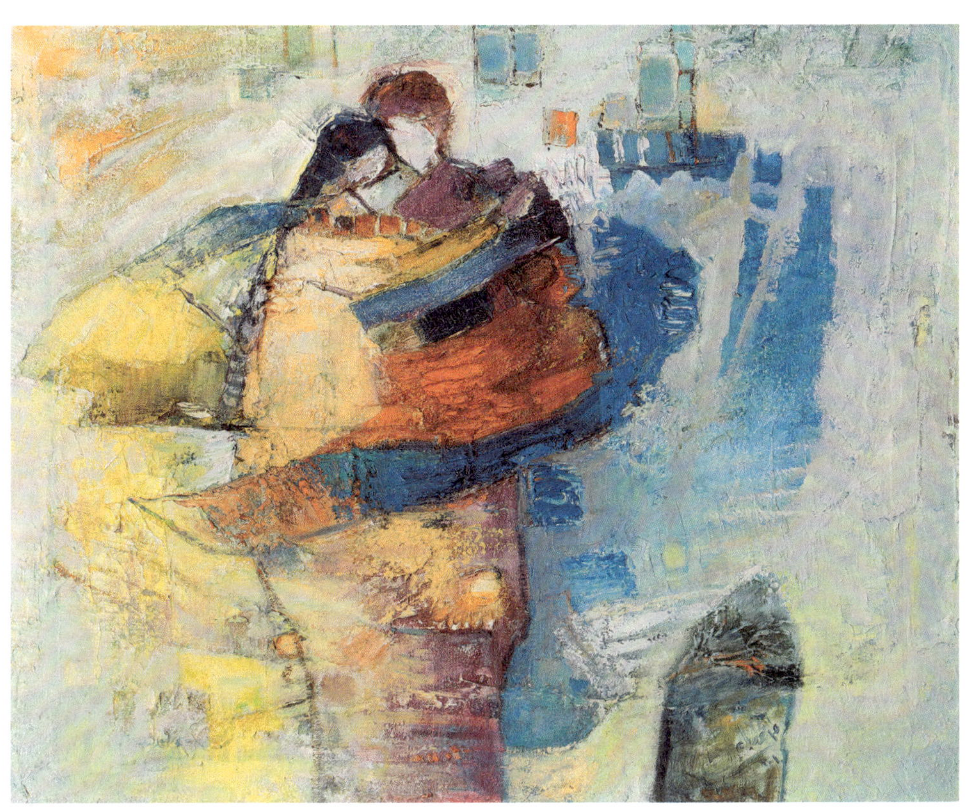

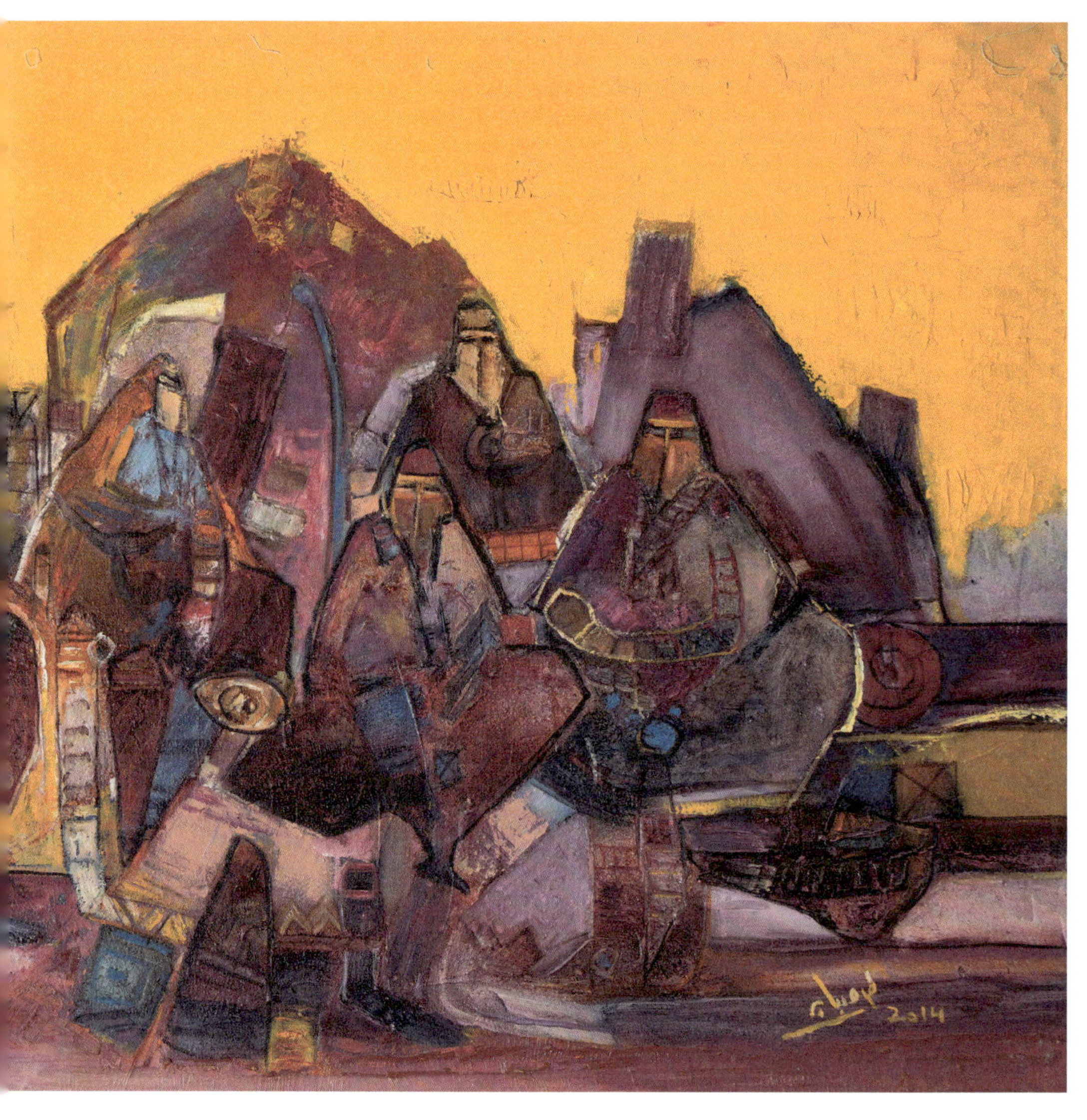

بدون عنوان، 2014

ألوان زيتية على قماش
100 × 200 سم
يإذن من الفنان

Untitled, 2014

Oil on canvas
100 × 200 cm
Courtesy of the artist

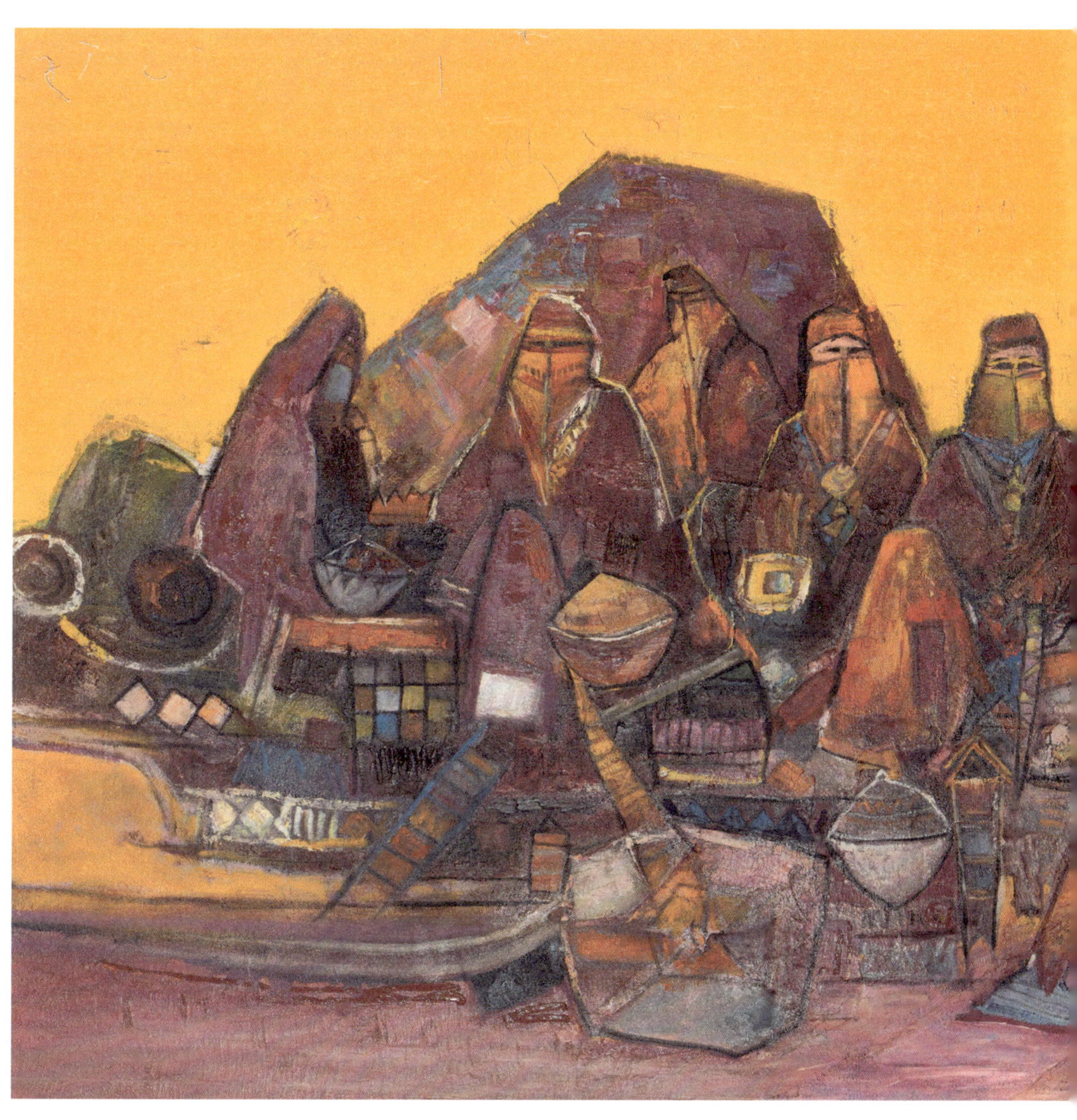

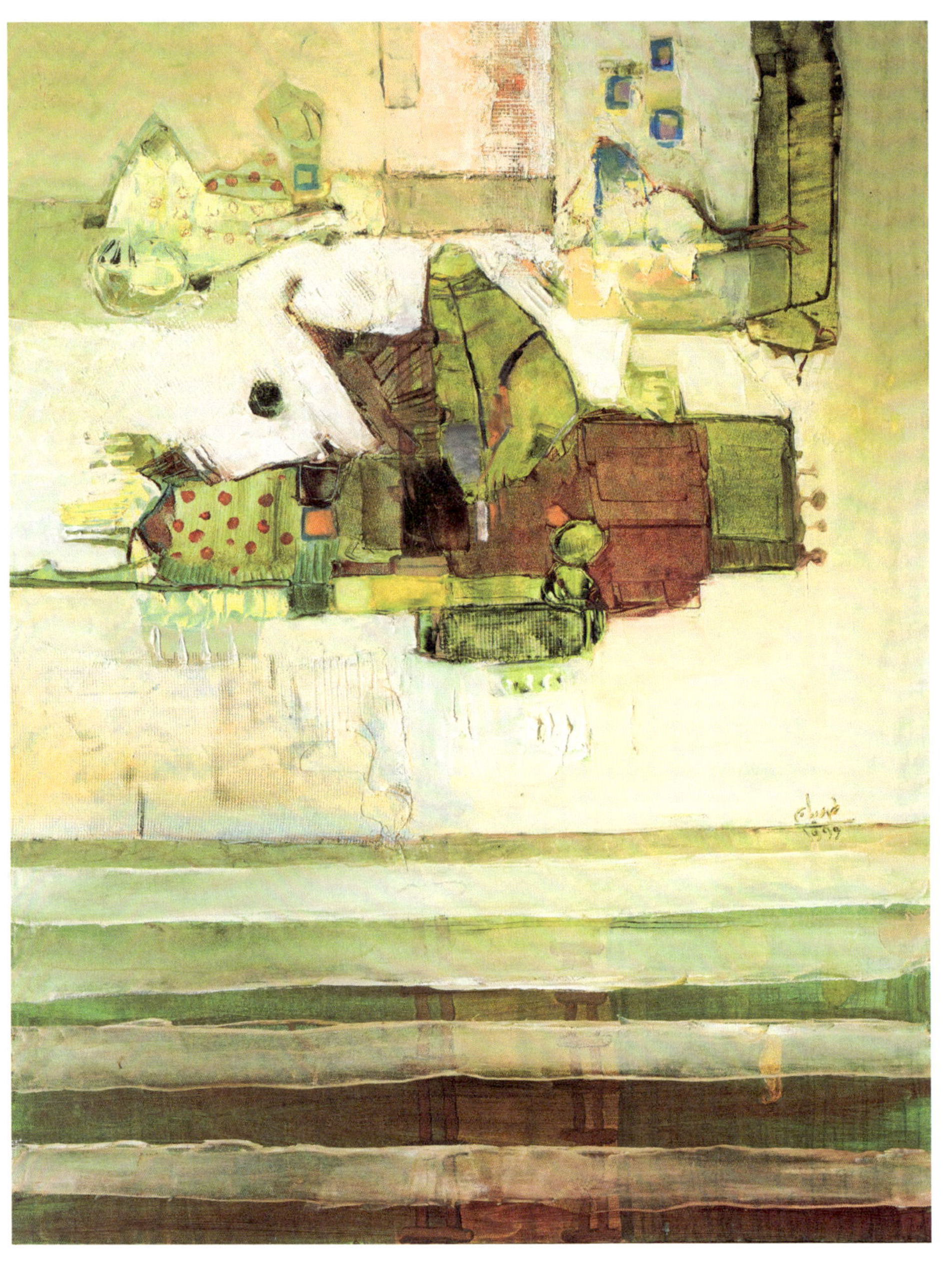

بدون عنوان، 1999

ألوان زيتية على قماش
100 × 80 سم
بإذن من الفنان

Untitled, 1999

Oil on canvas
100 × 80 cm
Courtesy of the artist

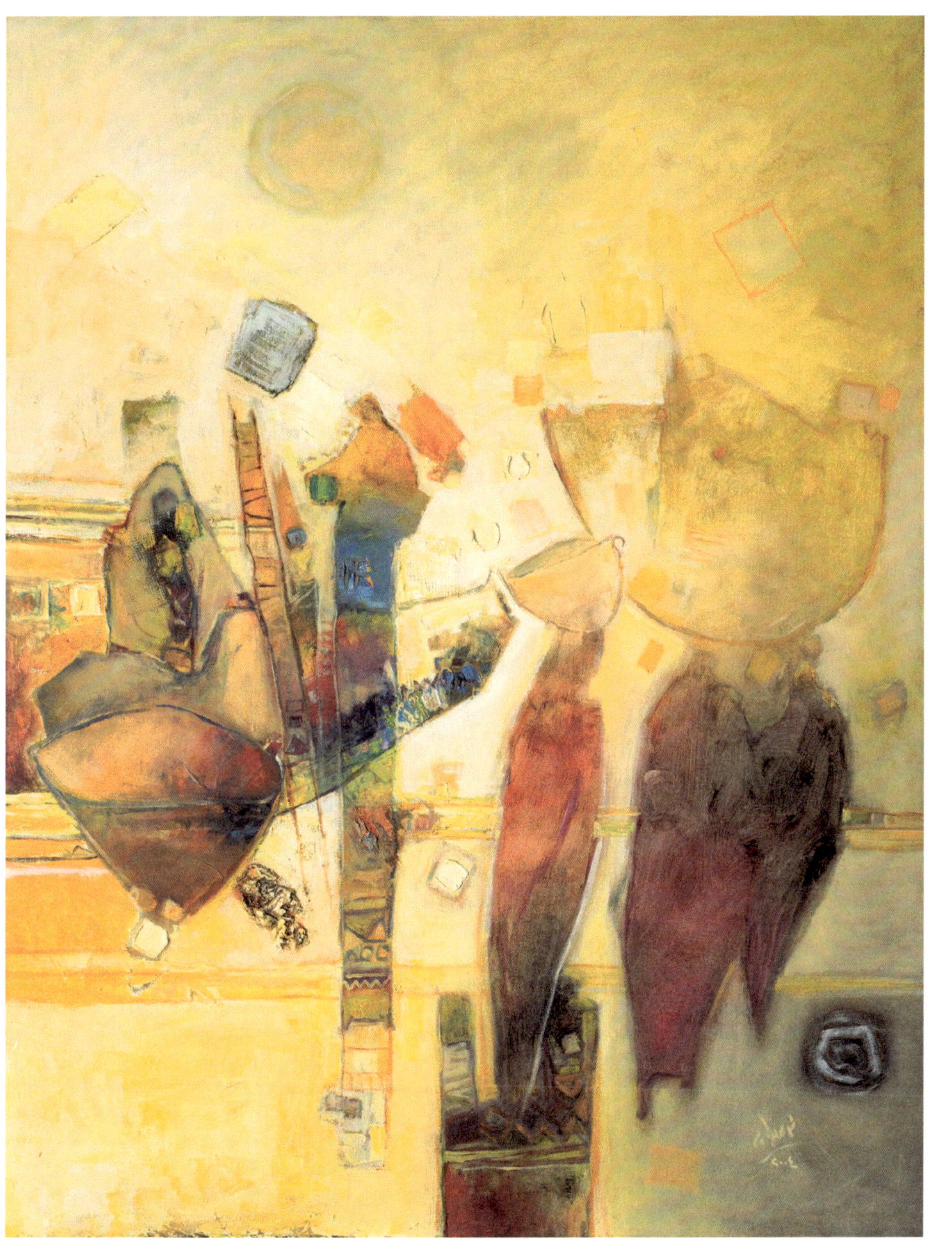

Untitled, 2004

Oil on canvas
122 × 91 cm
Courtesy of the artist

بدون عنوان، 2004

ألوان زيتية على قماش
122 × 91 سم
بإذن من الفنان

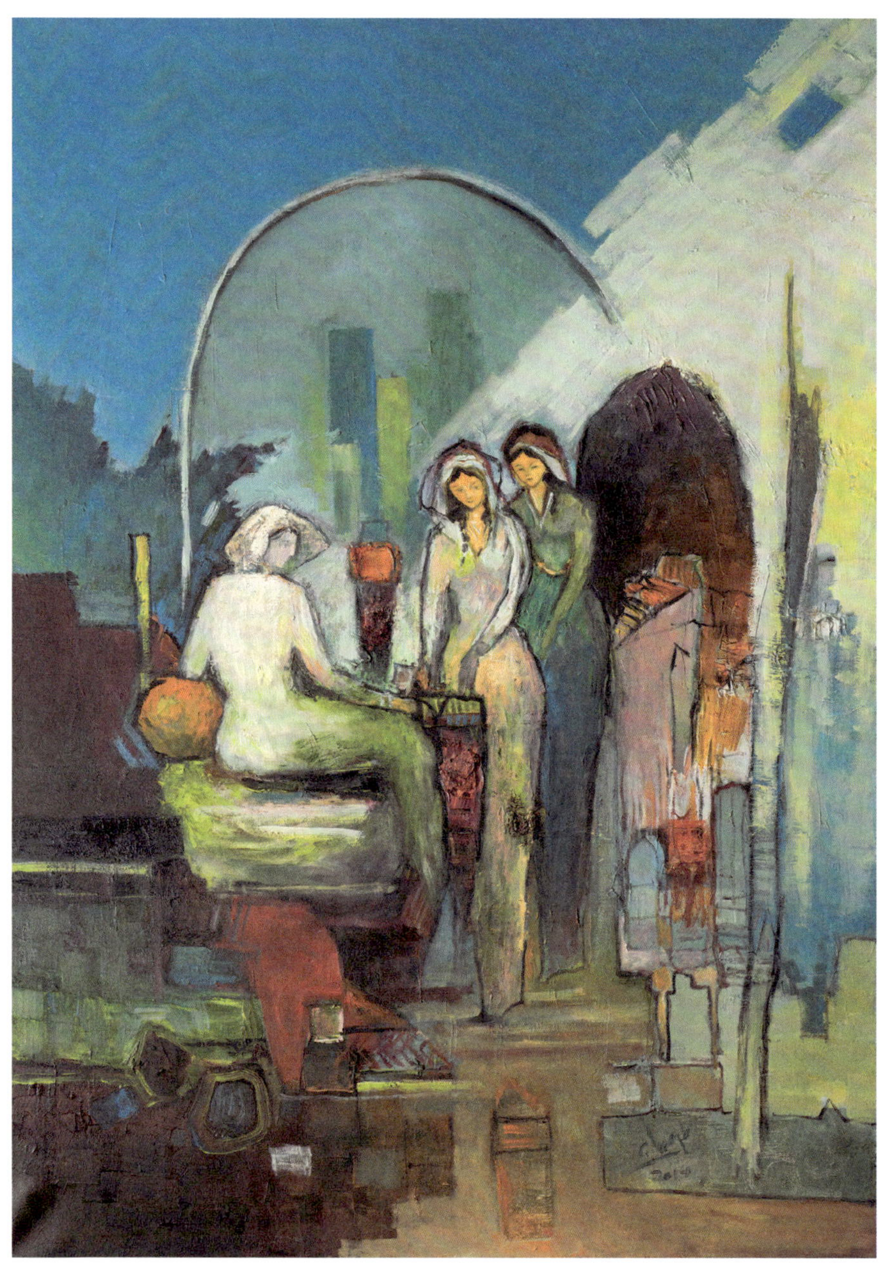

بدون عنوان، 2014

ألوان زيتية على قماش
106 × 76 سم
بإذن من الفنان

Untitled, 2014

Oil on canvas
106 × 76 cm
Courtesy of the artist

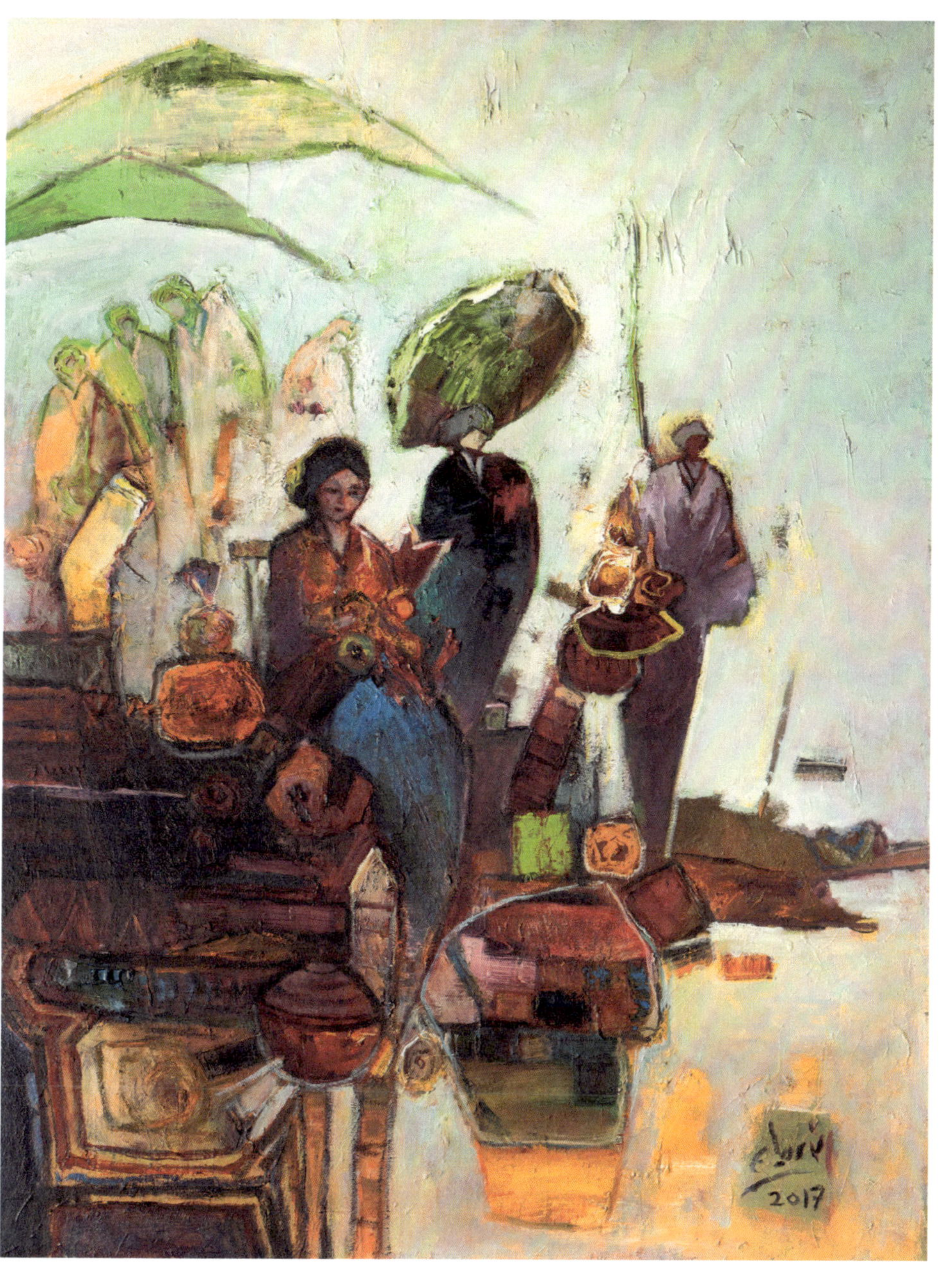

السوق، 2017

ألوان زيتية على قماش
76 × 101 سم
بإذن من الفنان

The Souq, 2017

Oil on canvas
101 × 76 cm
Courtesy of the artist

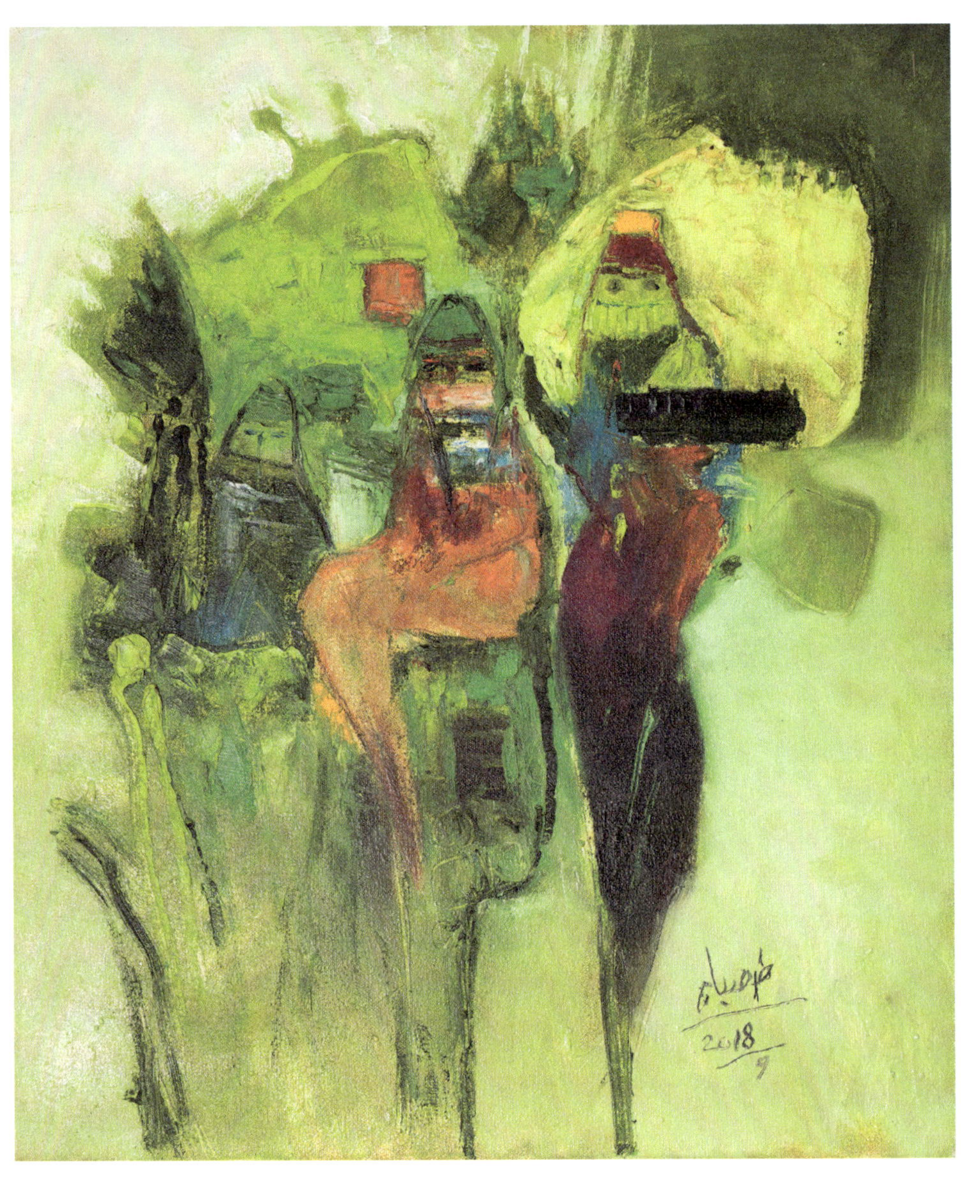

بدون عنوان، 2018

ألوان زيتية على قماش
63 × 76 سم
بإذن من الفنان

Untitled, 2018

Oil on canvas
76 × 63 cm
Courtesy of the artist

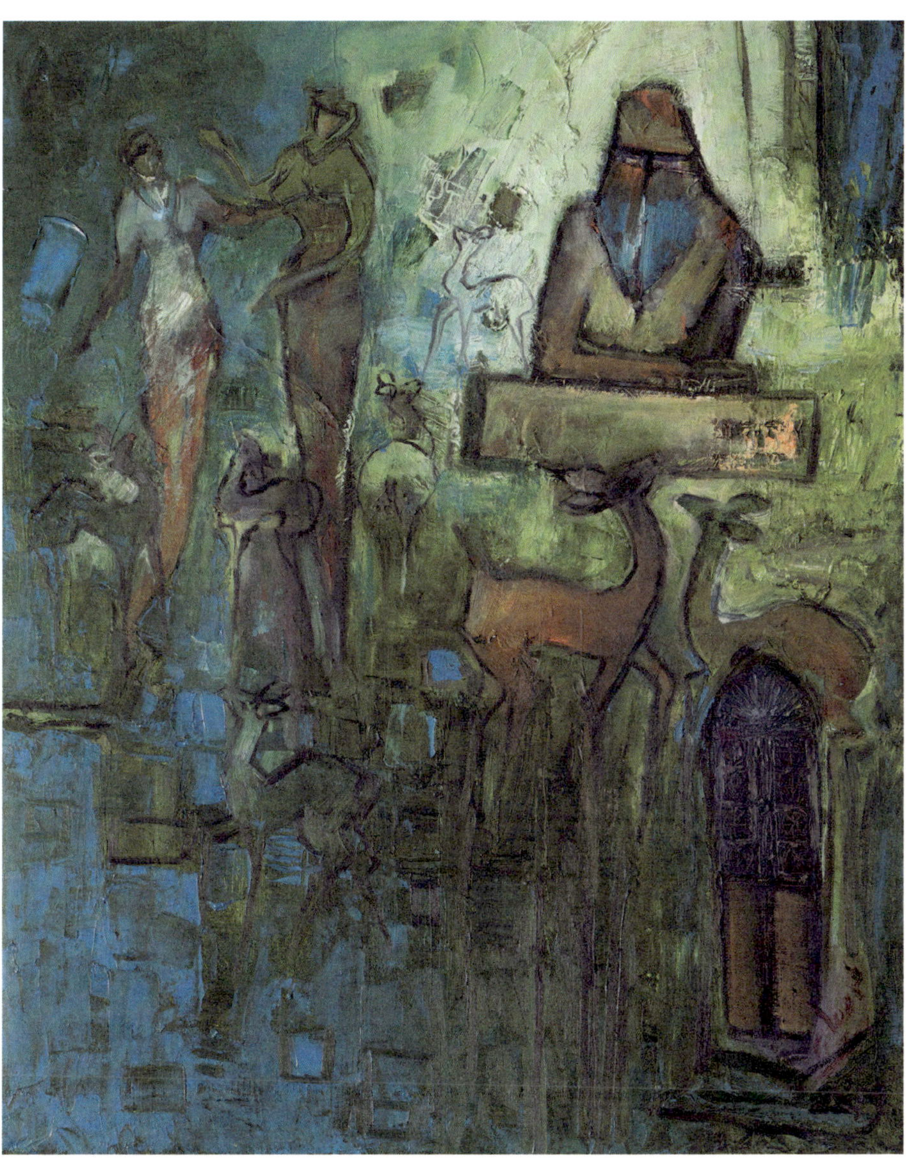

بدون عنوان، 2019

ألوان زيتية على قماش
70 × 50 سم
بإذن من الفنان

Untitled, 2019

Oil on canvas
70 × 50 cm
Courtesy of the artist

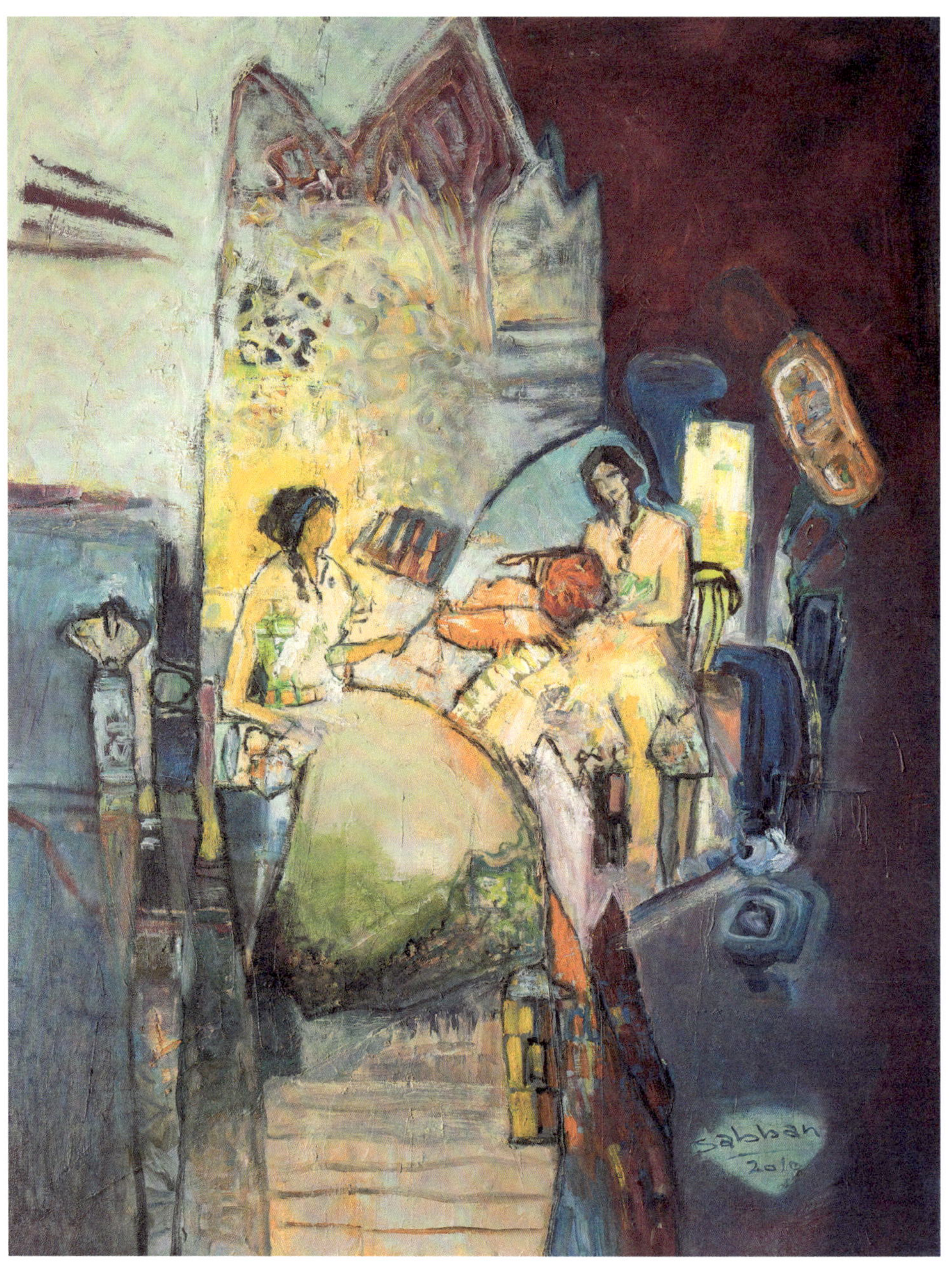

بدون عنوان، 2019

ألوان زيتية على قماش
76 × 101 سم
بإذن من الفنان

Untitled, 2019

Oil on canvas
101 × 76 cm
Courtesy of the artist

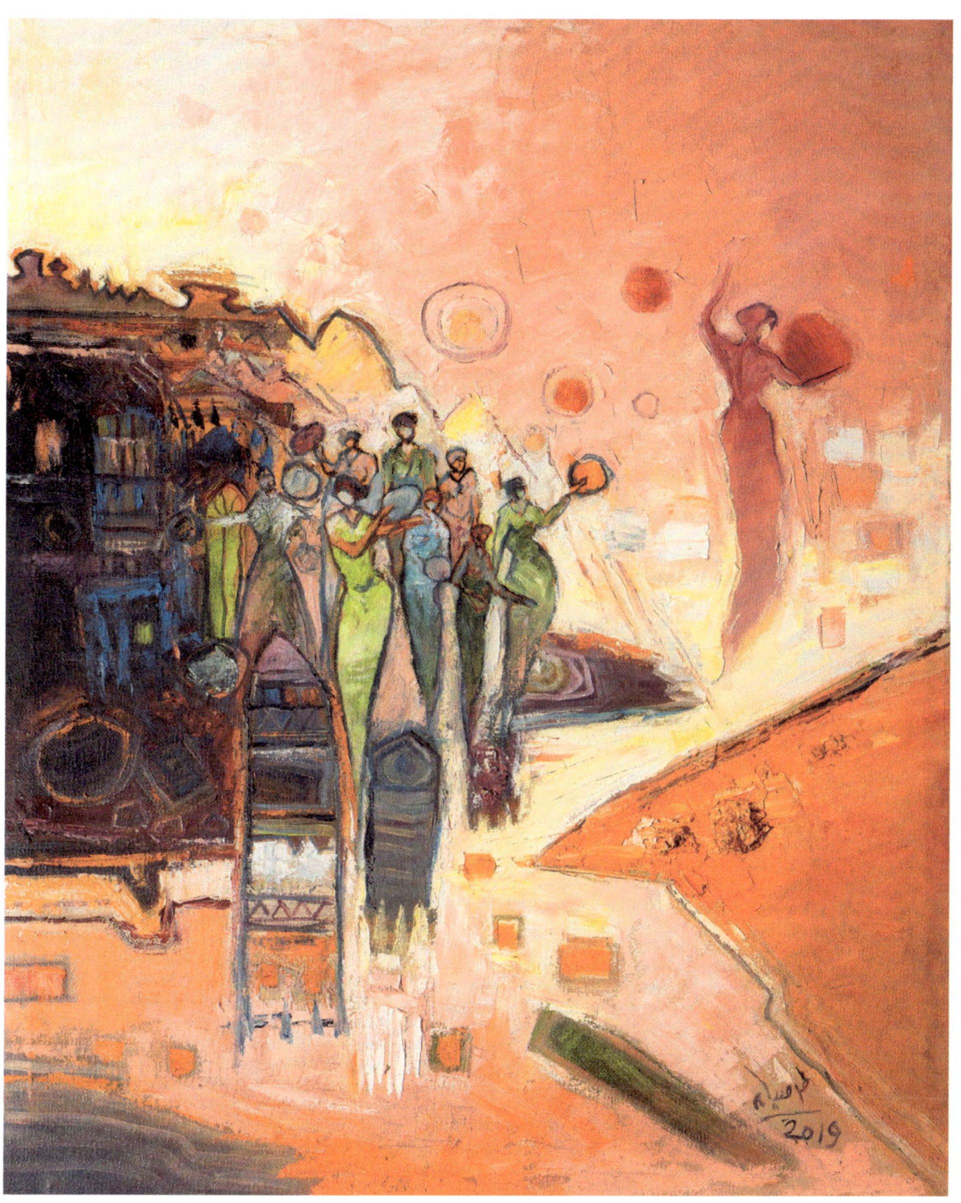

Untitled, 2019

Oil on canvas
100 × 80 cm
Courtesy of the artist

بدون عنوان، 2019

ألوان زيتية على قماش
100 × 80 سم
بإذن من الفنان

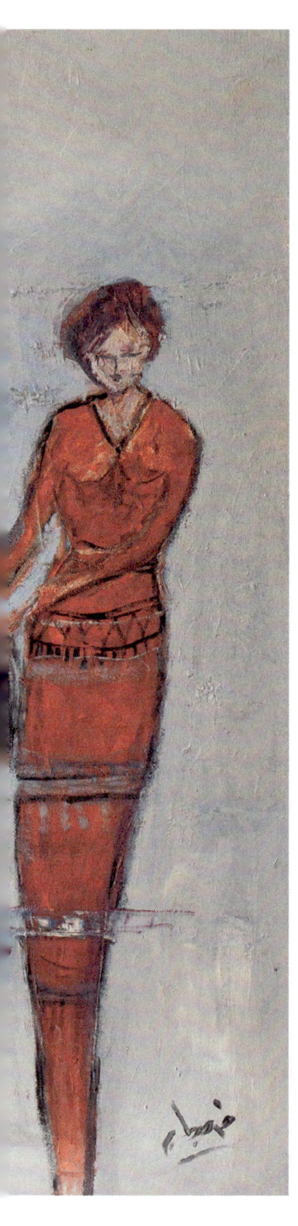

بدون عنوان، 2020

ألوان زيتية على قماش
100 × 120 سم
بإذن من الفنان

Untitled, 2020

Oil on canvas
100 × 120 cm
Courtesy of the artist

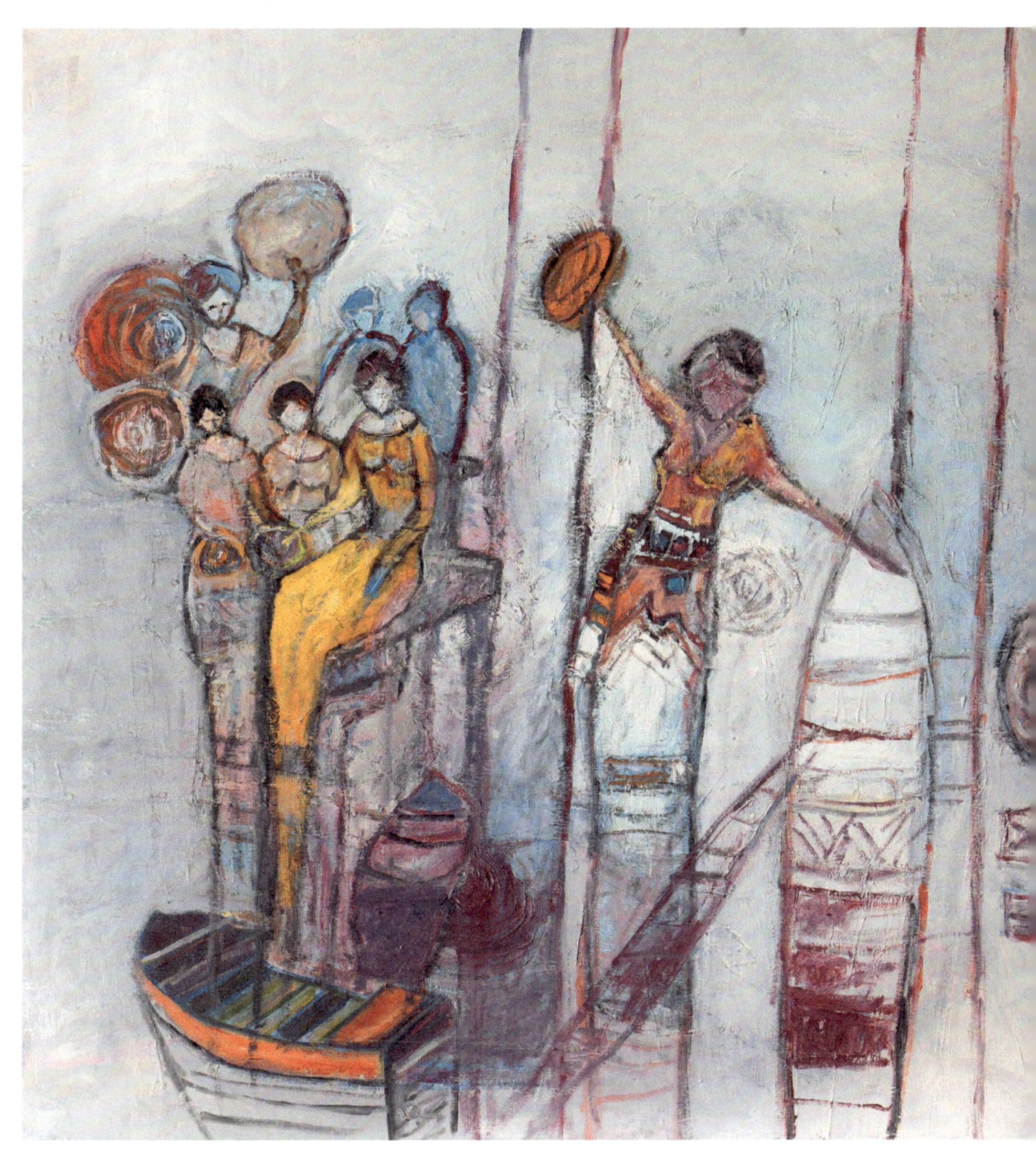

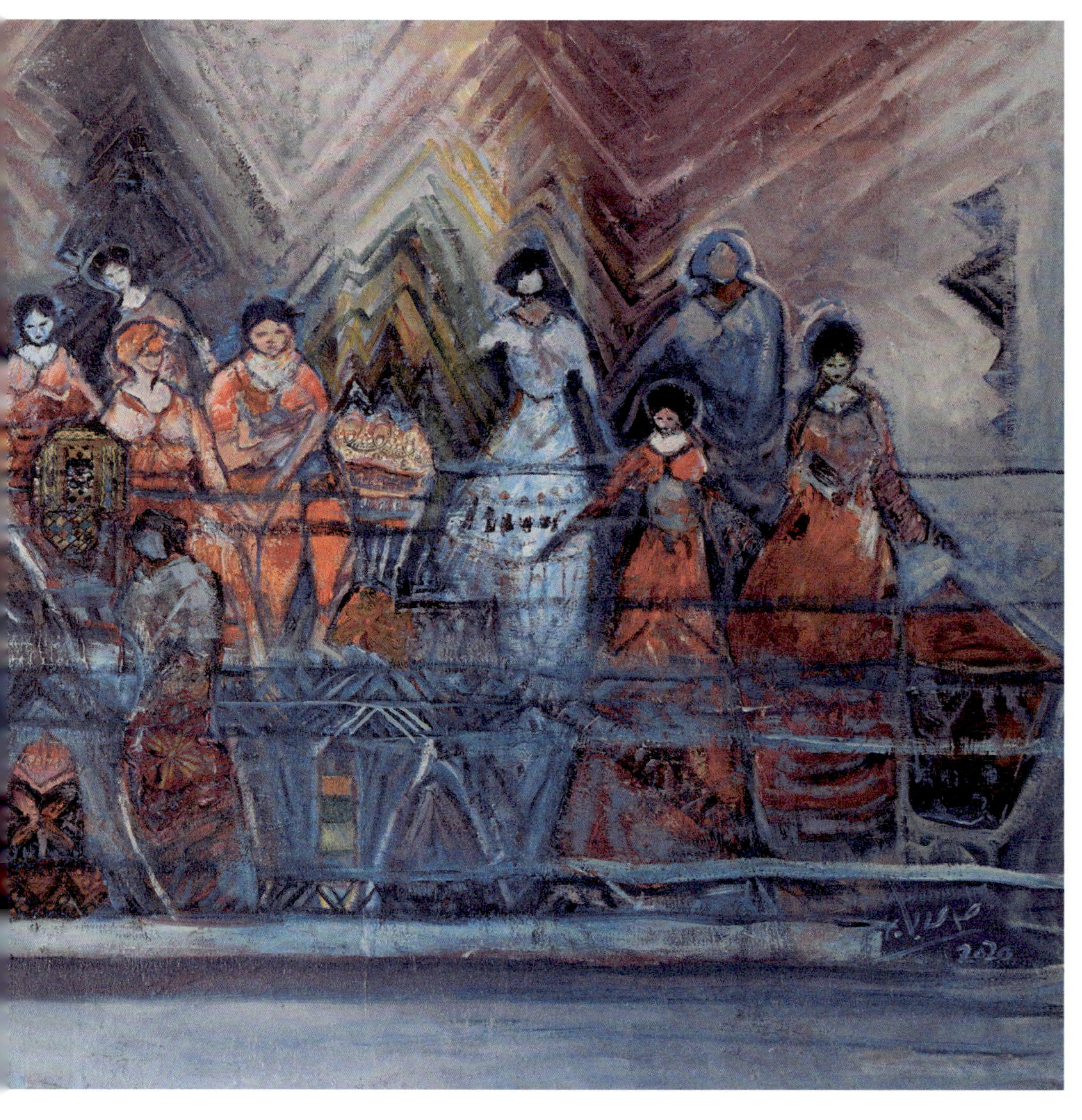

Women's Discourse, 2020

ألوان زيتية على قماش
100 × 200 سم
بإذن من الفنان

Oil on canvas
100 × 200 cm
Courtesy of the artist

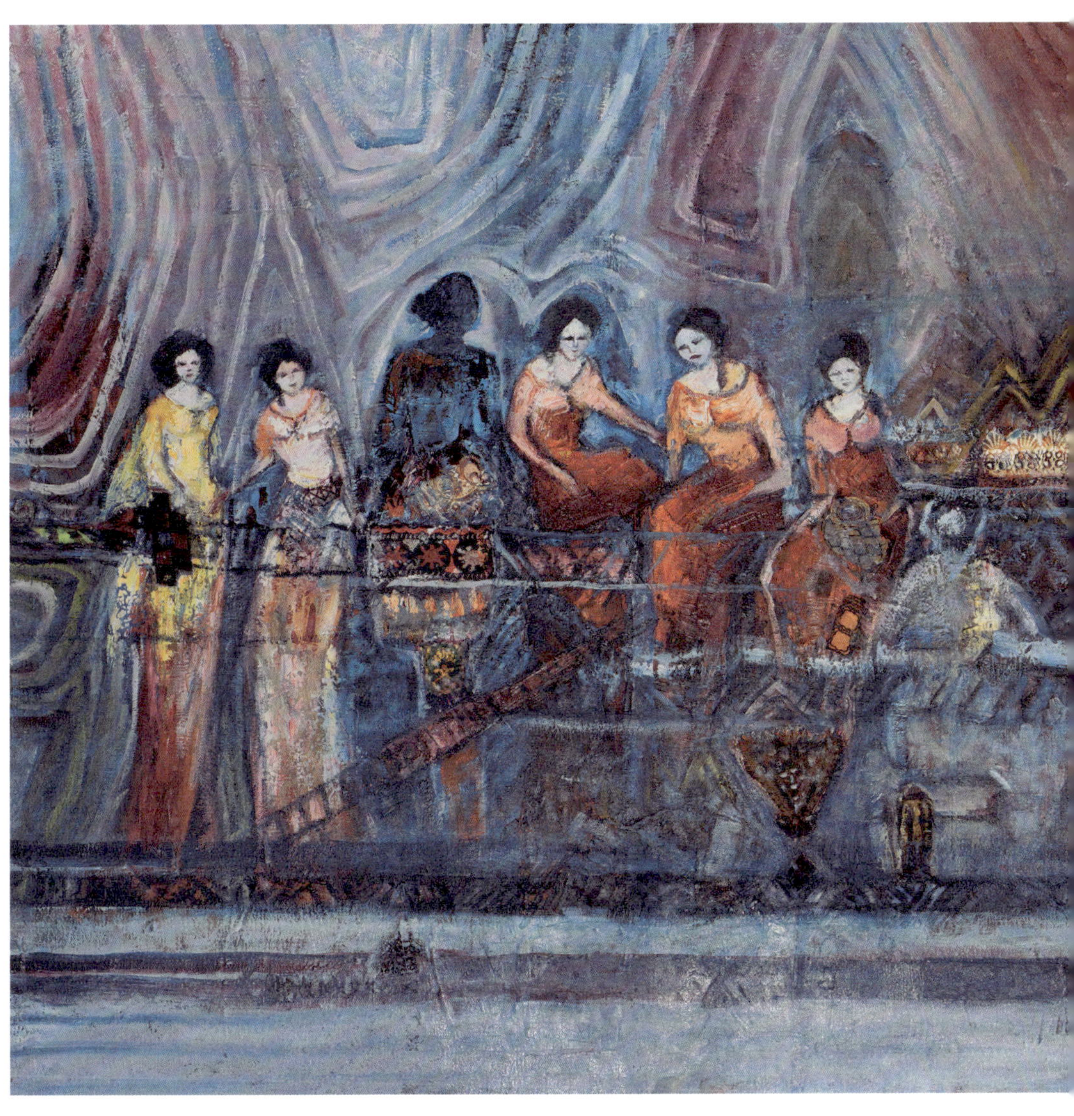

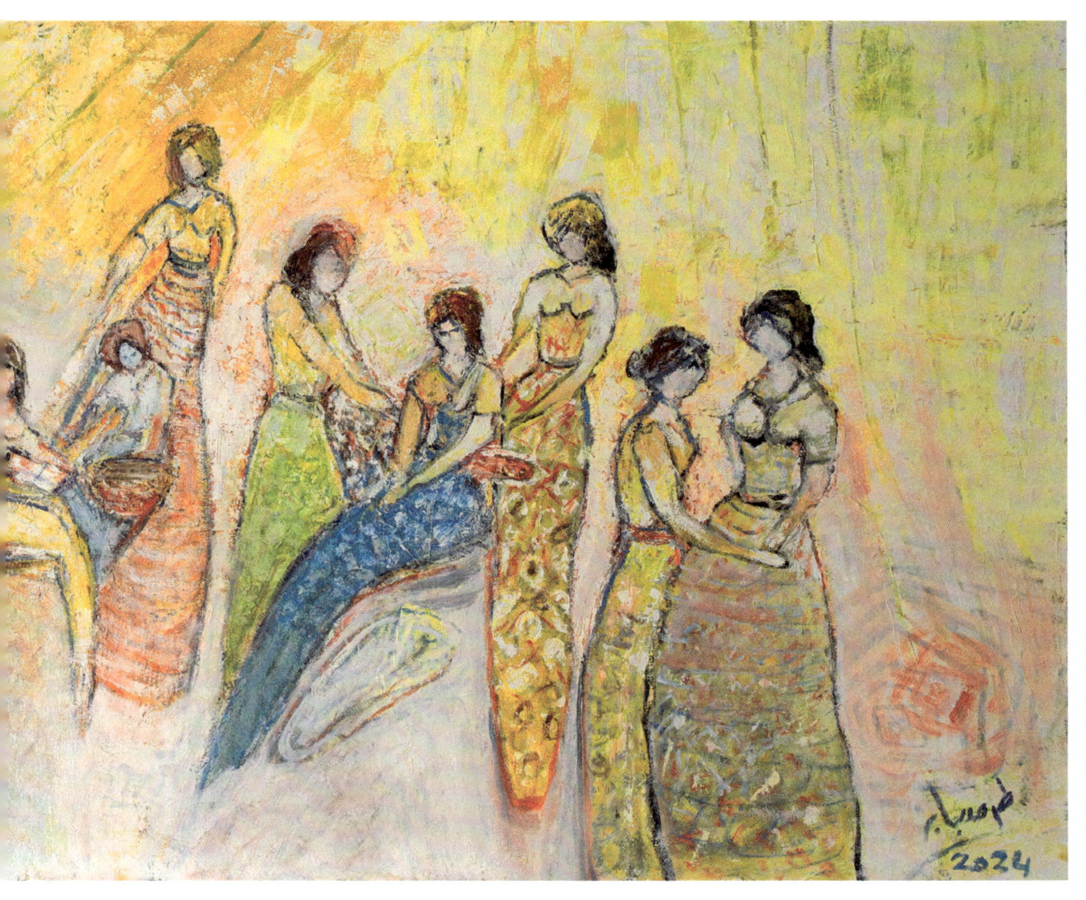

فرح، 2024

ألوان زيتية على قماش
100 × 250 سم
بإذن من الفنان

Festivity, 2024

Oil on canvas
100 × 250 cm
Courtesy of the artist

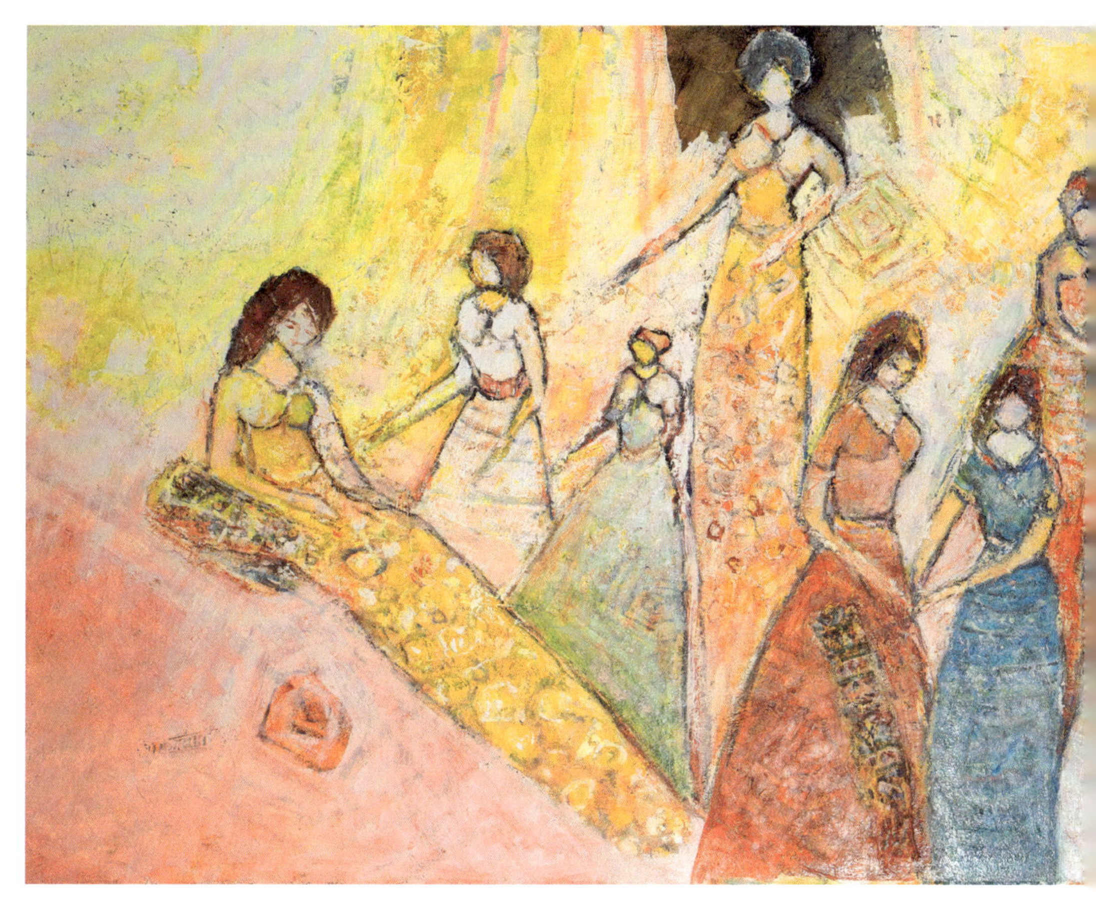

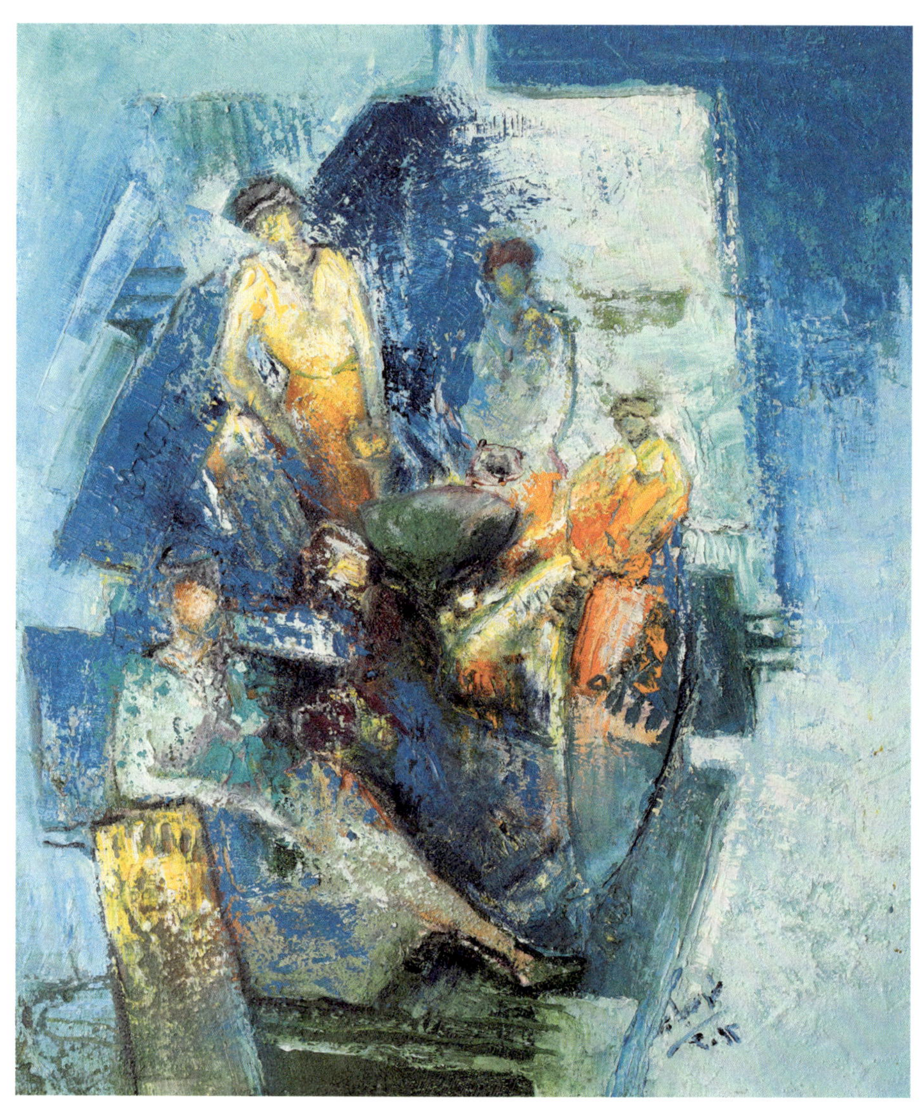

بدون عنوان، 2012

ألوان زيتية على قماش
60 × 50 سم
بإذن من الفنان

Untitled, 2012

Oil on canvas
60 × 50 cm
Courtesy of the artist

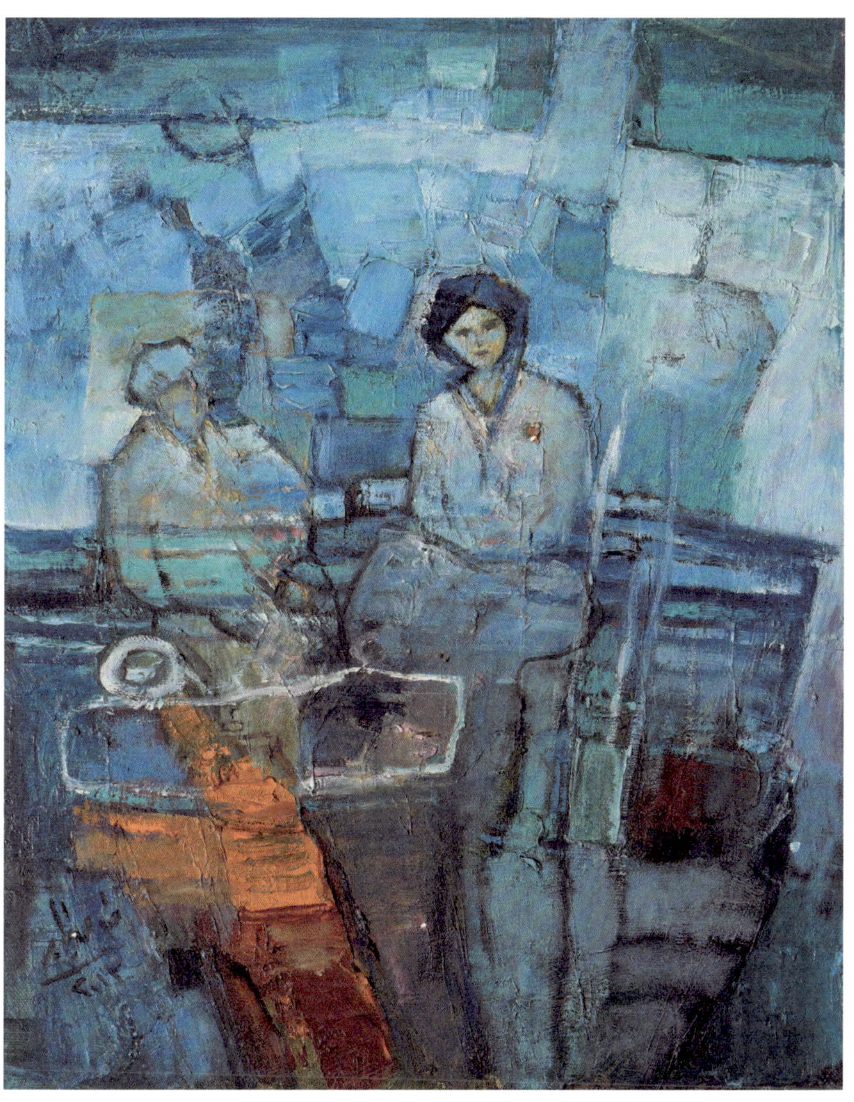

Untitled, 2013

Oil on canvas
46 × 35 cm
Courtesy of the artist

بدون عنوان، 2013

ألوان زيتية على قماش
46 × 35 سم
بإذن من الفنان

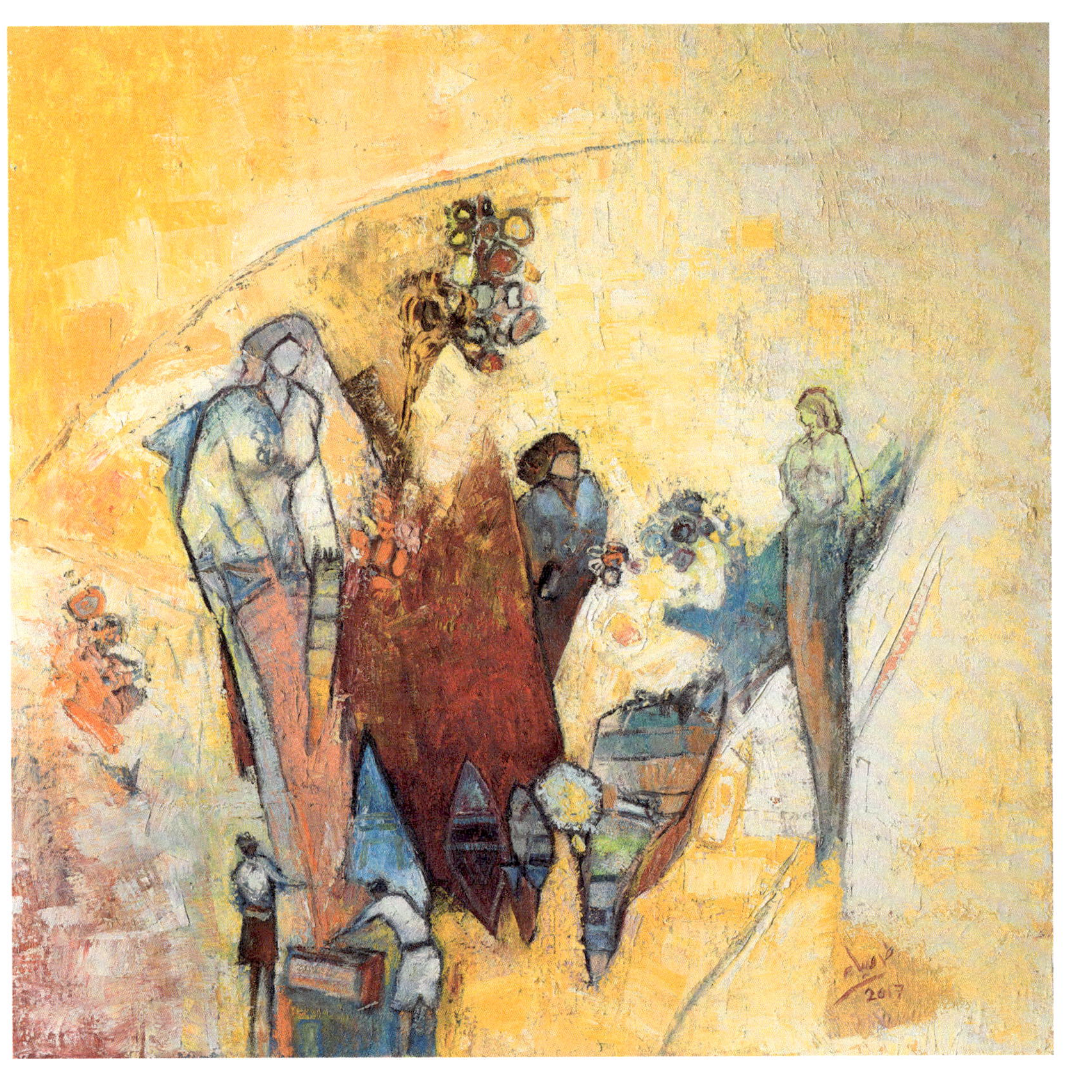

بحر الأصفر، 2017

ألوان زيتية على قماش
100 × 100 سم
بإذن من الفنان

Yellow Sea, 2017

Oil on canvas
100 × 100 cm
Courtesy of the artist

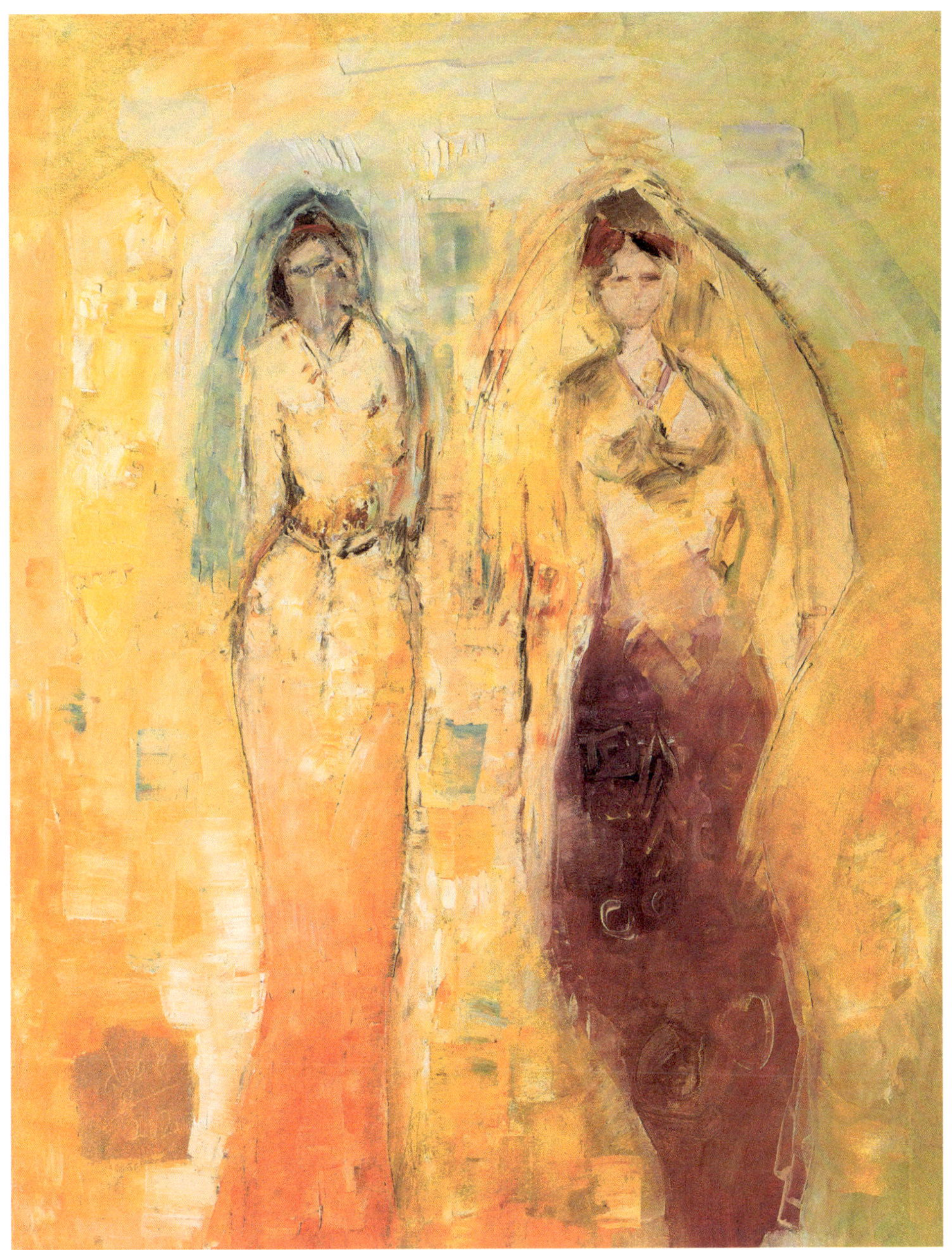

بدون عنوان، 2020

ألوان زيتية على قماش
101 × 76 سم
بإذن من الفنان

Untitled, 2020

Oil on canvas
101 × 76 cm
Courtesy of the artist

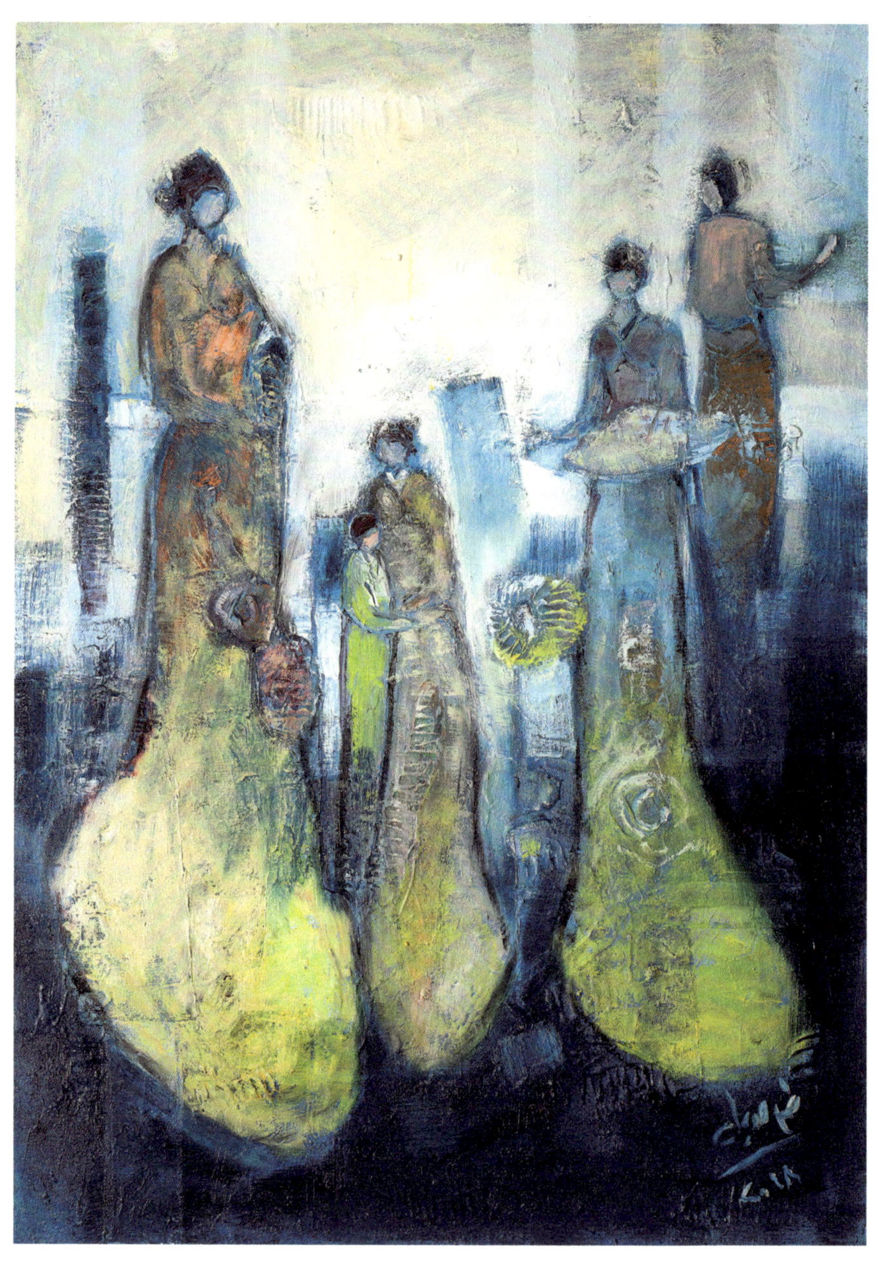

بدون عنوان، 2018

ألوان زيتية على قماش
100 × 70 سم
بإذن من الفنان

Untitled, 2018

Oil on canvas
100 × 70 cm
Courtesy of the artist

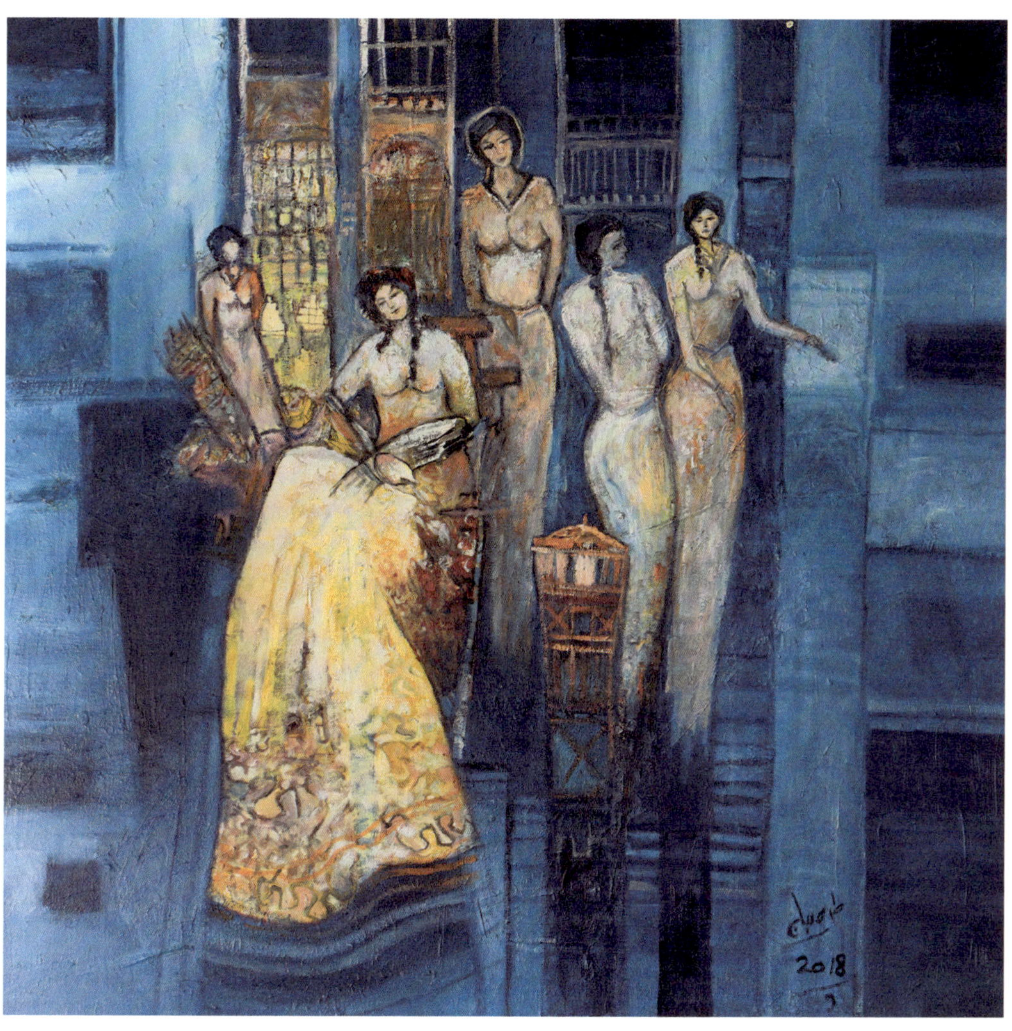

بدون عنوان، 2018

ألوان زيتية على قماش
120 × 120 سم
بإذن من الفنان

Untitled, 2018

Oil on canvas
120 × 120 cm
Courtesy of the artist

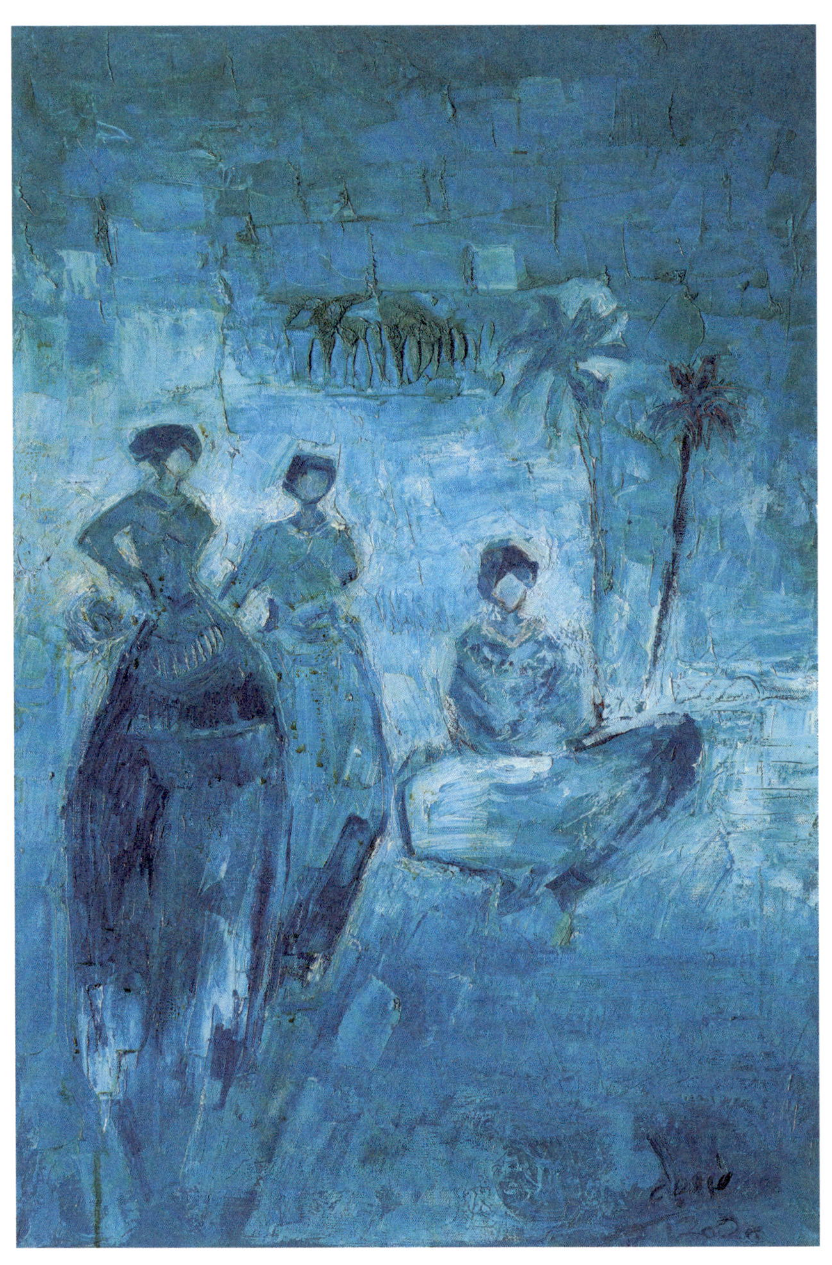

Serene, 2020

Oil on canvas
76 × 51 cm
Courtesy of the artist

سكون، 2020

ألوان زيتية على قماش
76 × 51 سم
بإذن من الفنان

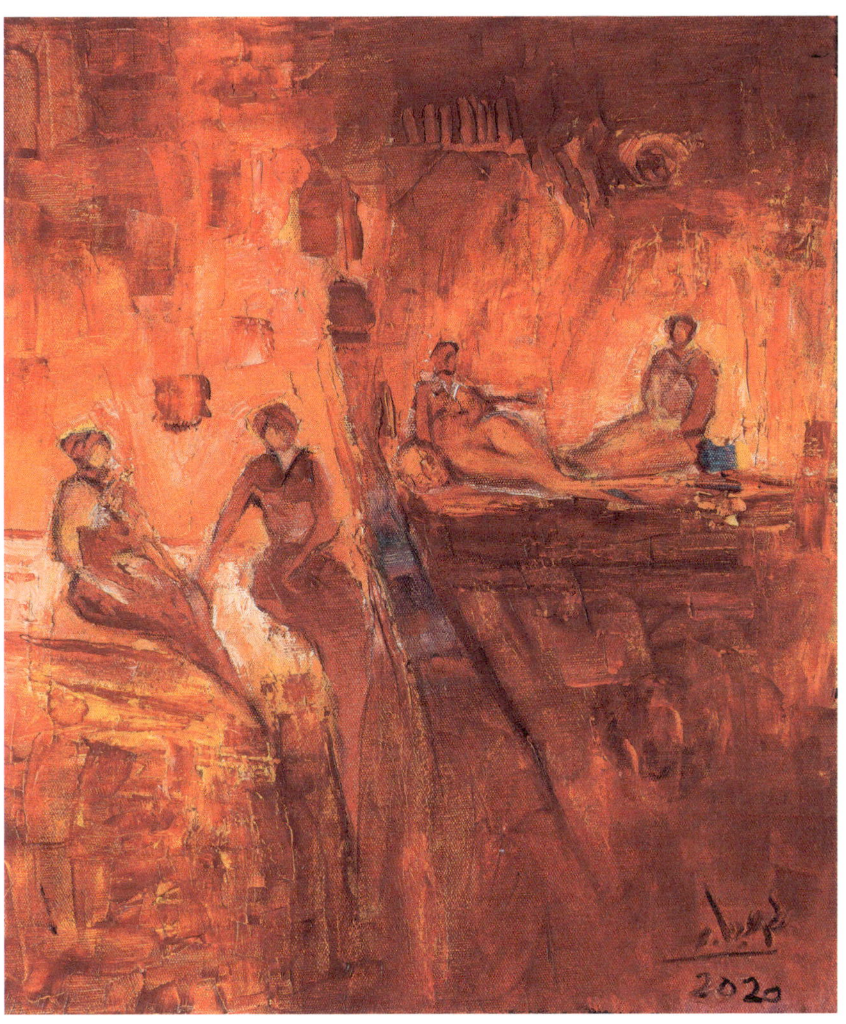

بدون عنوان، 2020

ألوان زيتية على قماش
50 × 40 سم
بإذن من الفنان

Untitled, 2020

Oil on canvas
50 × 40 cm
Courtesy of the artist

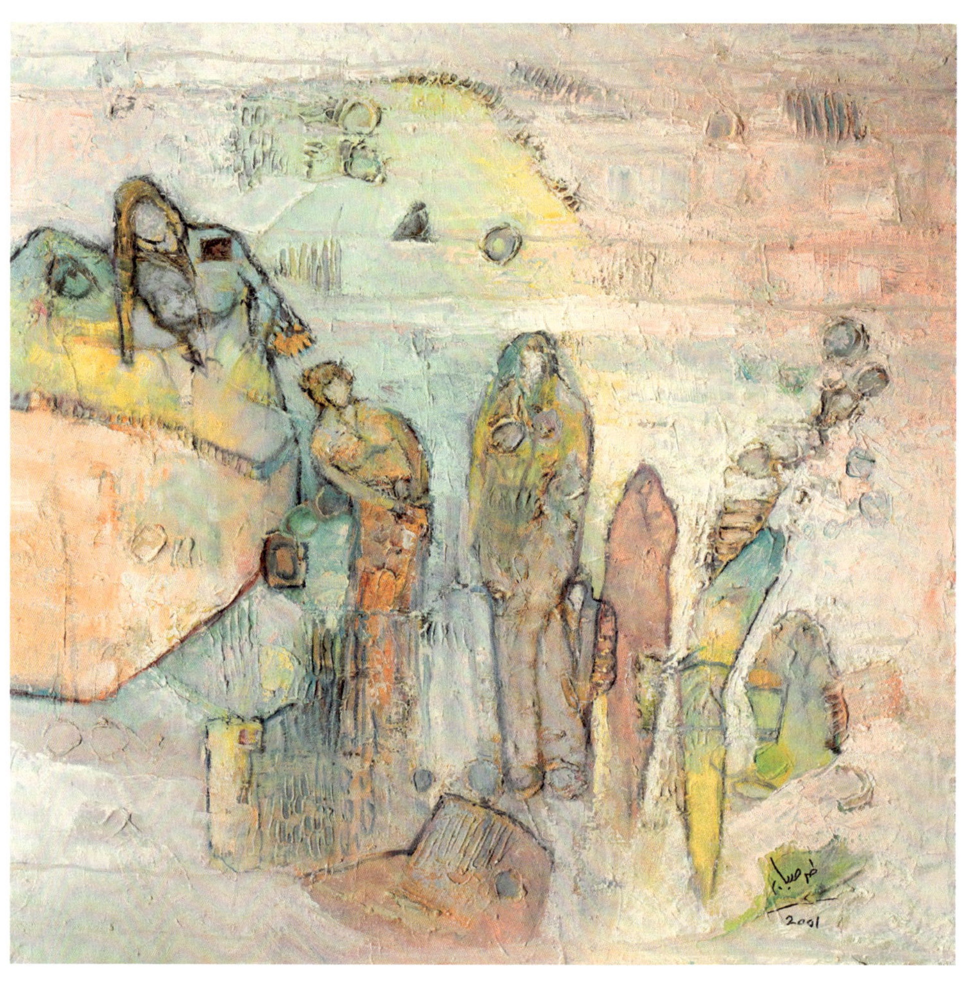

بدون عنوان، 2001

ألوان زيتية على قماش
80 × 80 سم
بإذن من الفنان

Untitled, 2001

Oil on canvas
80 × 80 cm
Courtesy of the artist

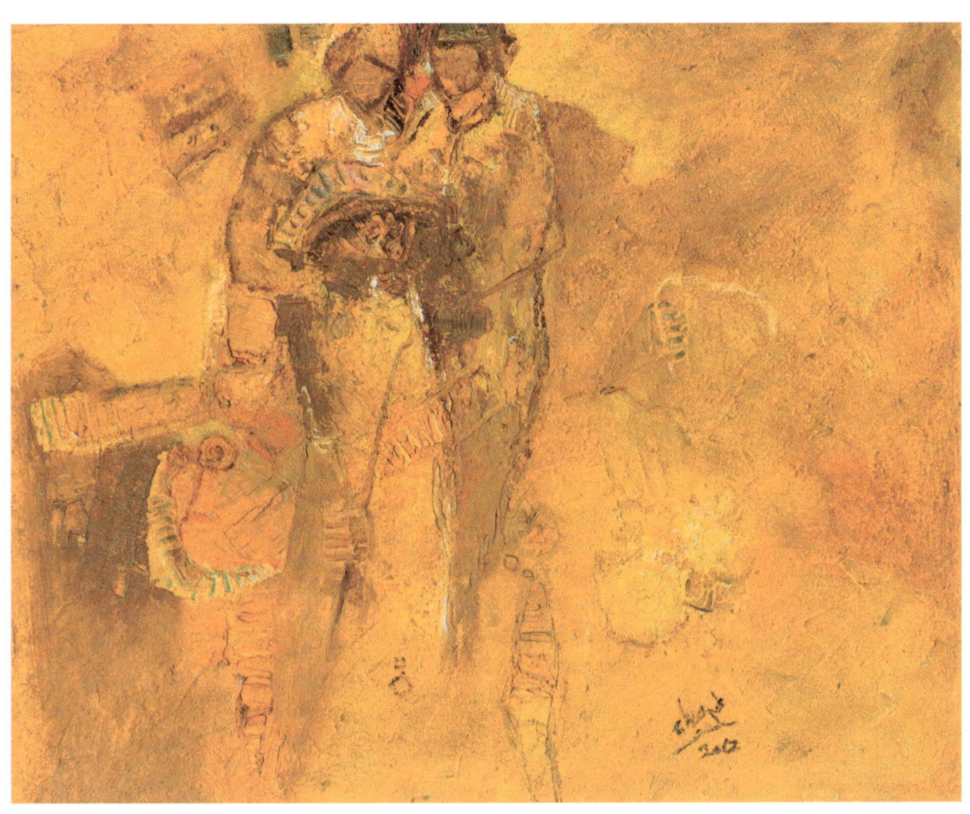

بدون عنوان، 2012

ألوان زيتية على قماش
50 × 60 سم
بإذن من الفنان

Untitled, 2012

Oil on canvas
50 × 60 cm
Courtesy of the artist

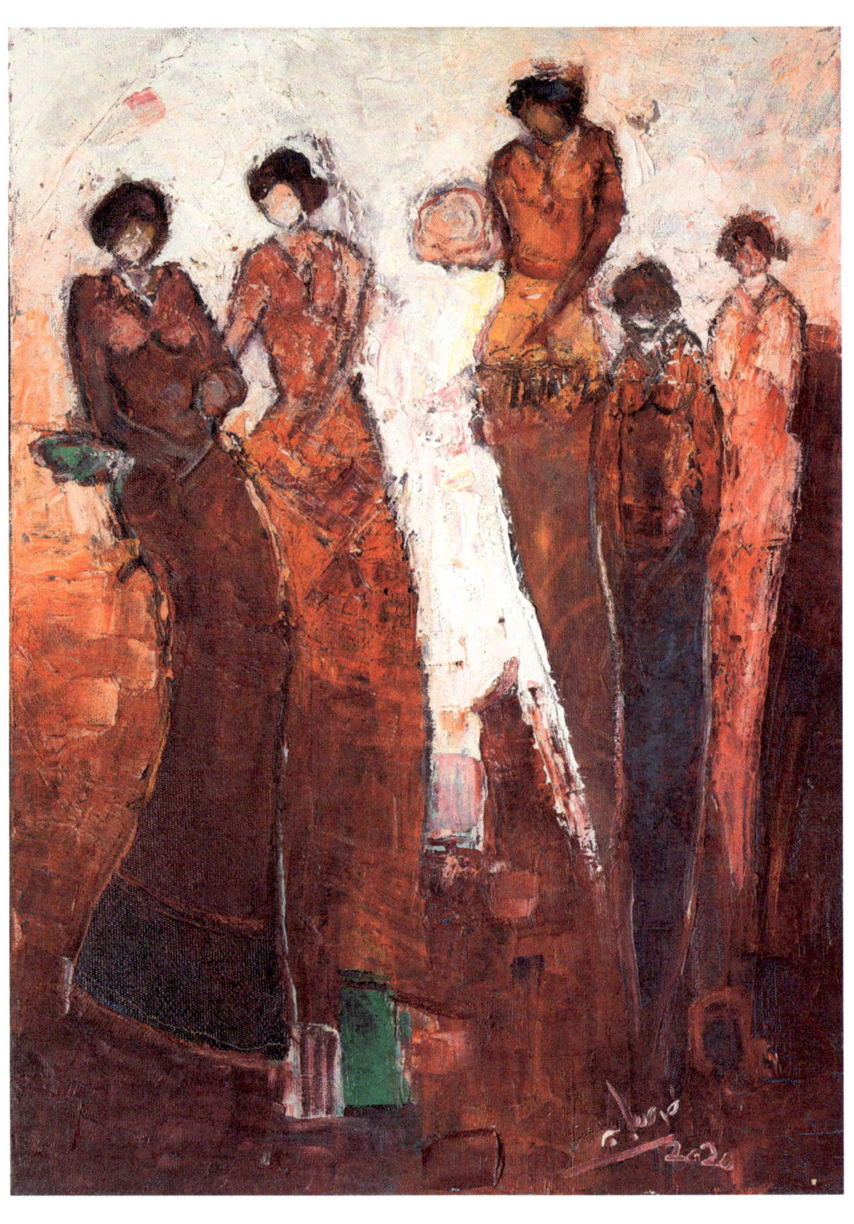

Festivities, 2020

Oil on canvas
60 × 50 cm
Courtesy of the artist

احتفال، 2020

ألوان زيتية على قماش
60 × 50 سم
بإذن من الفنان

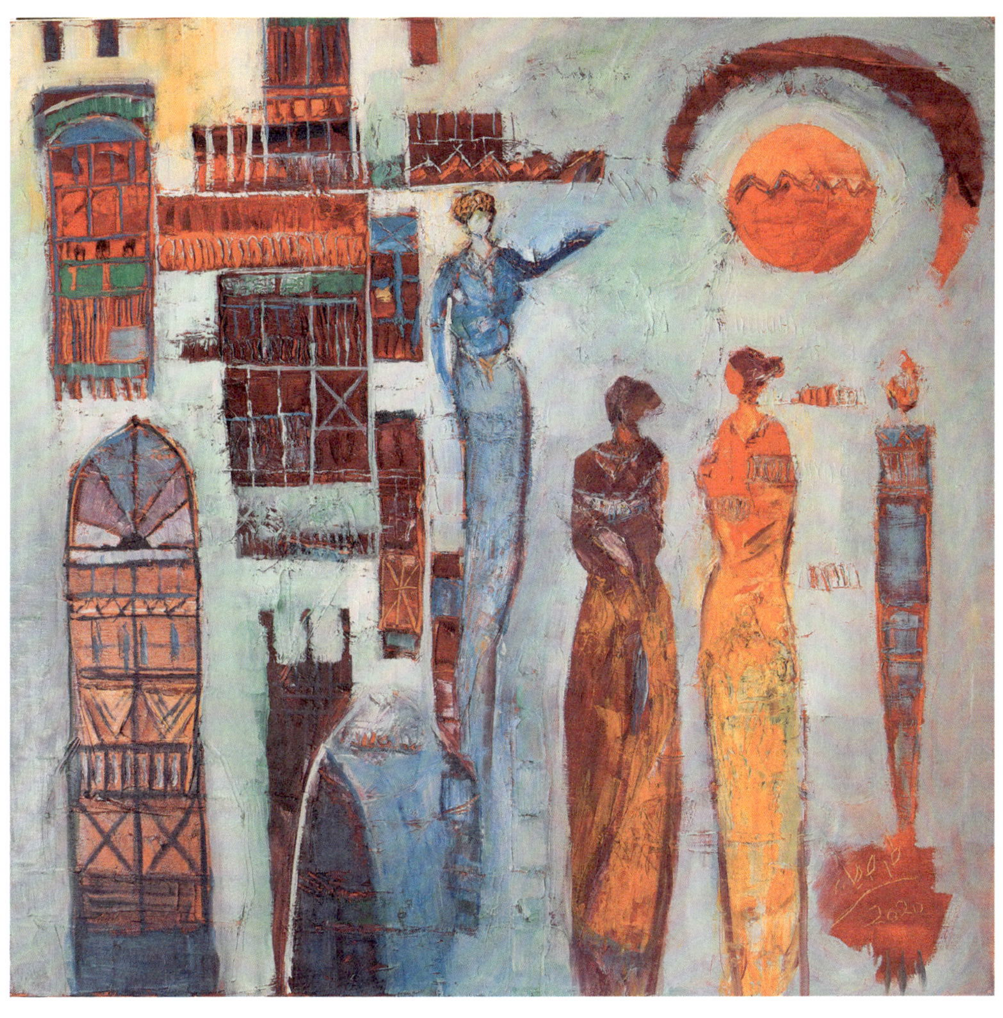

بدون عنوان، 2020

ألوان زيتية على قماش
80 × 80 سم
بإذن من الفنان

Untitled, 2020

Oil on canvas
80 × 80 cm
Courtesy of the artist

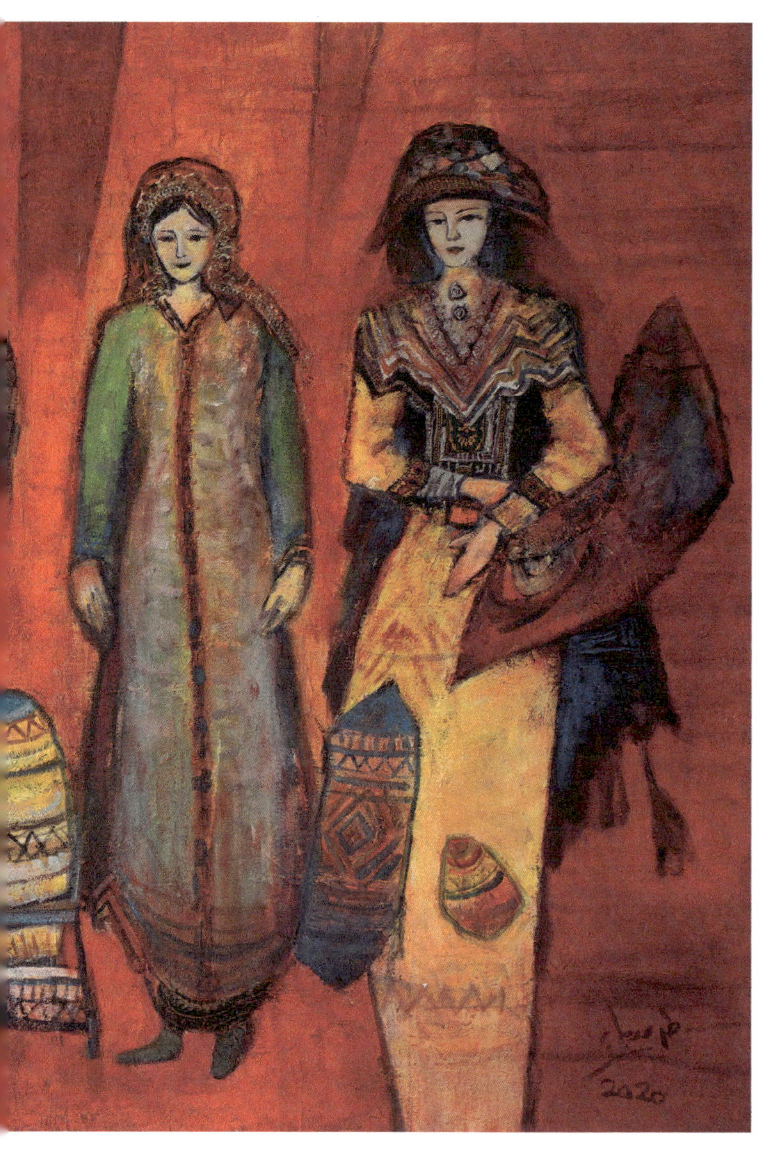

الزي التقليدي، 2020

ألوان زيتية ونسيج على قماش
120 × 200 سم
بإذن من الفنان

Traditional Attire, 2020

Oil and fabric on canvas
120 × 200 cm
Courtesy of the artist

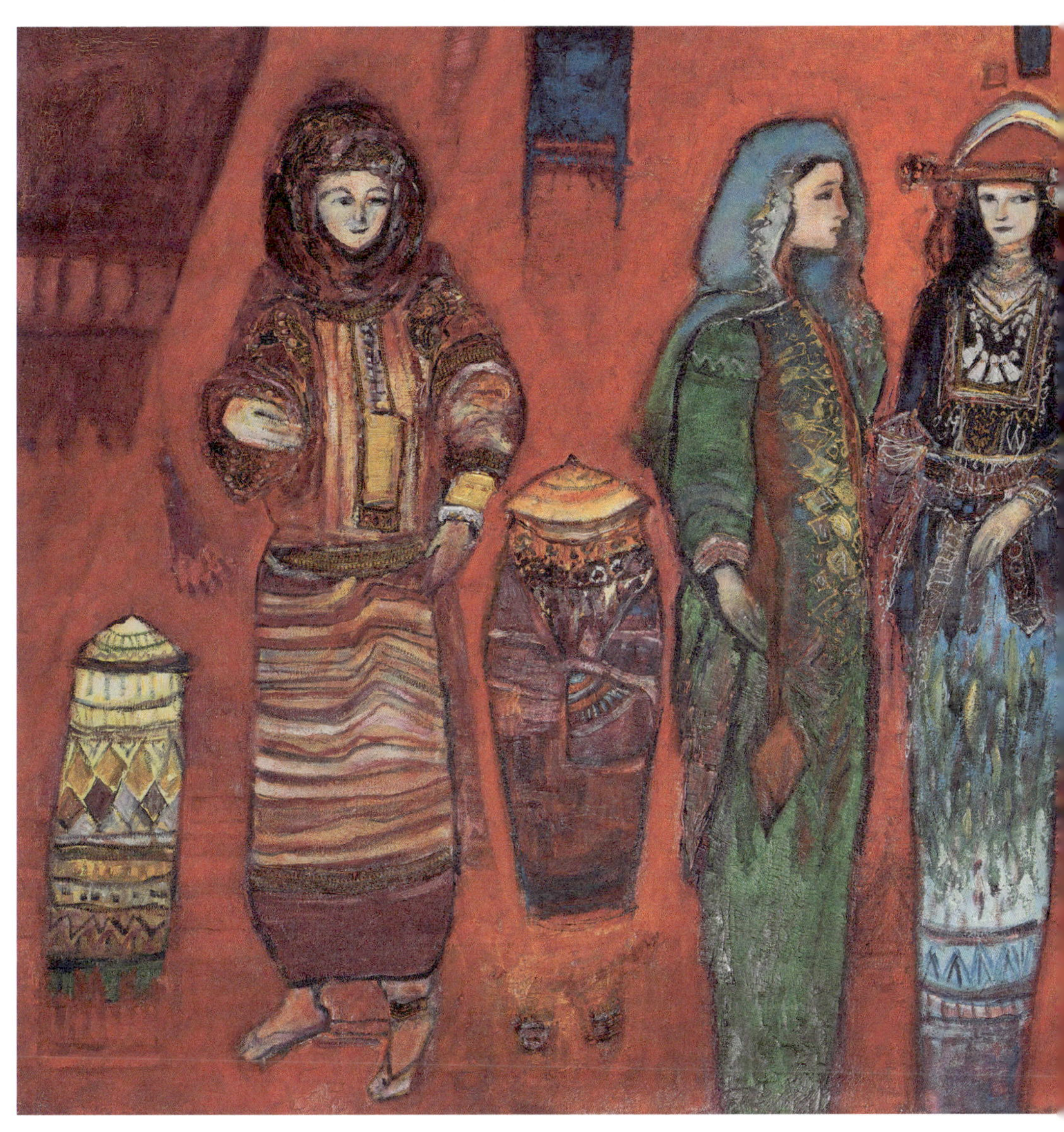

ألوان زيتية ونسيج على قماش
120 × 100 سم
بإذن من الفنان

Building, 2020

Oil and fabric on canvas
120 × 100 cm
Courtesy of the artist

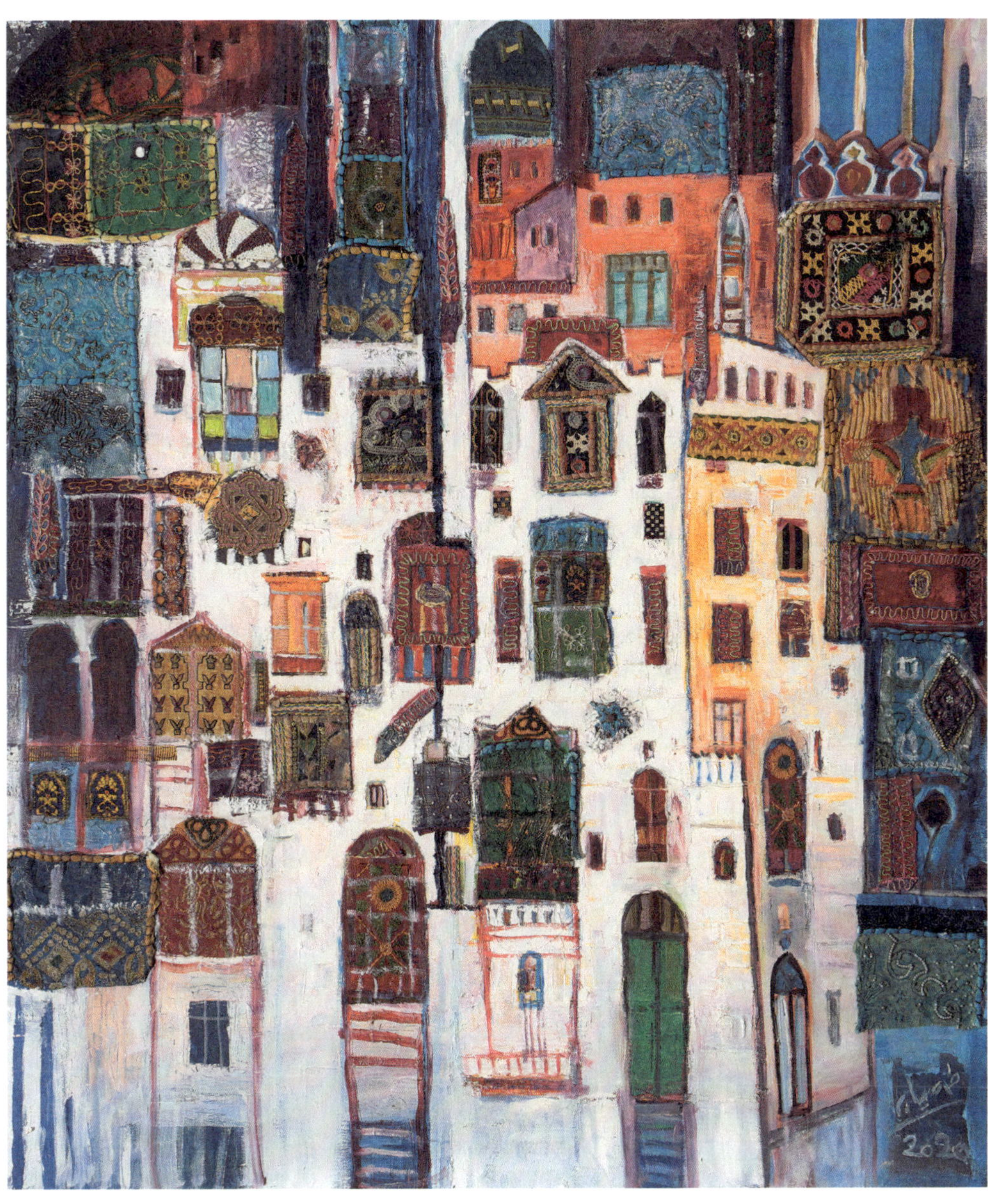

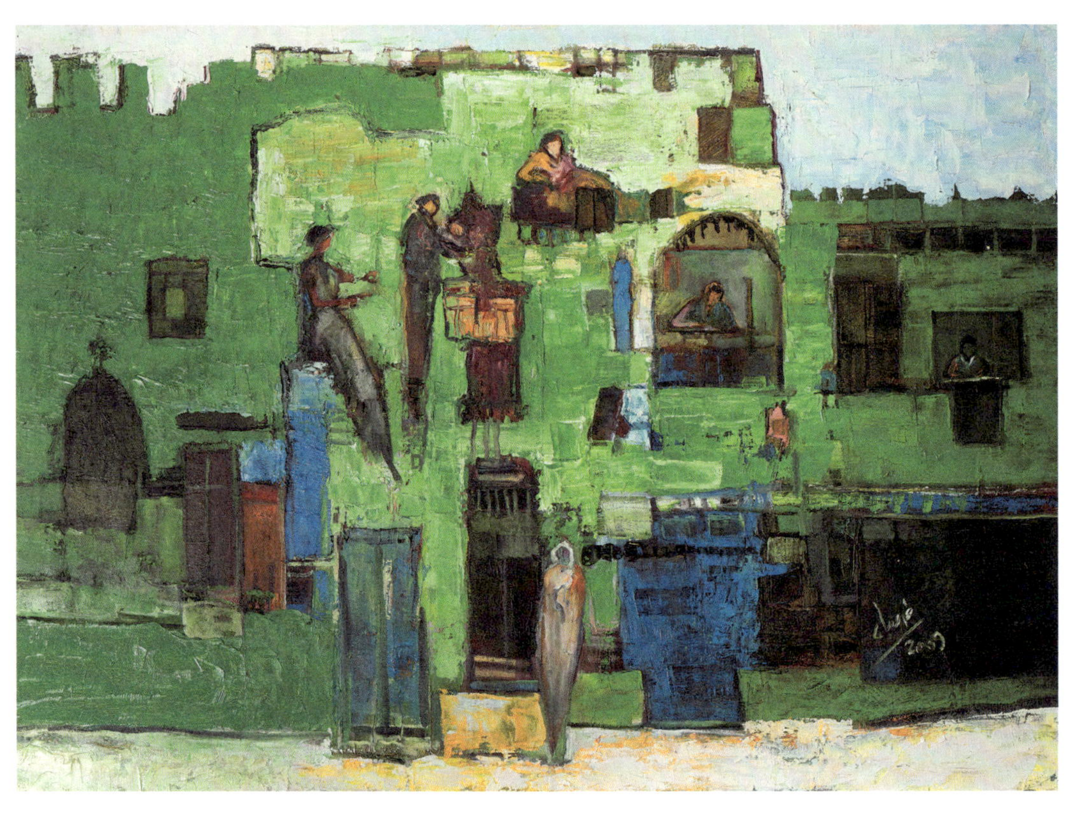

Green, 2009

Oil on canvas
76 × 100 cm
Courtesy of the artist

أخضر، 2009

ألوان زيتية على قماش
76 × 100 سم
بإذن من الفنان

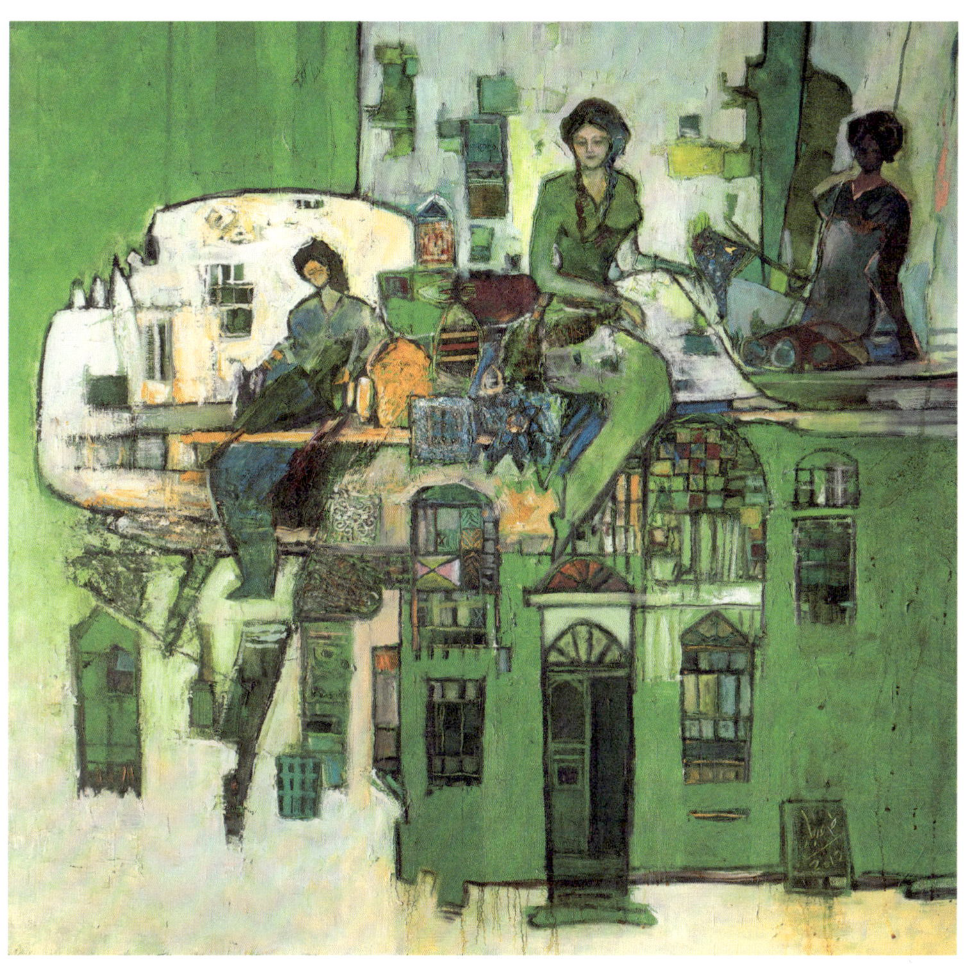

روح المدينة، 2012

ألوان زيتية على قماش
100 × 100 سم
بإذن من الفنان

Spirit of the City, 2012

Oil on canvas
100 × 100 cm
Courtesy of the artist

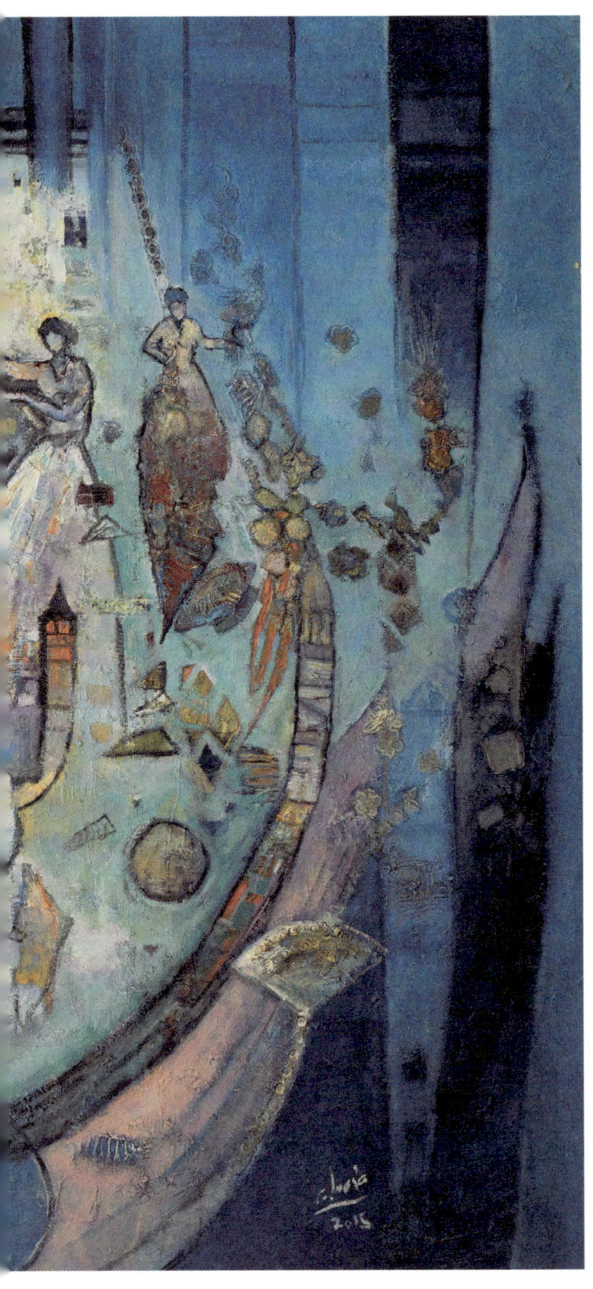

حياة حجازية، 2015

ألوان زيتية على قماش
150 × 200 سم
يإذن من الفنان

Hijazi Life, 2015

Oil on canvas
150 × 200 cm
Courtesy of the artist

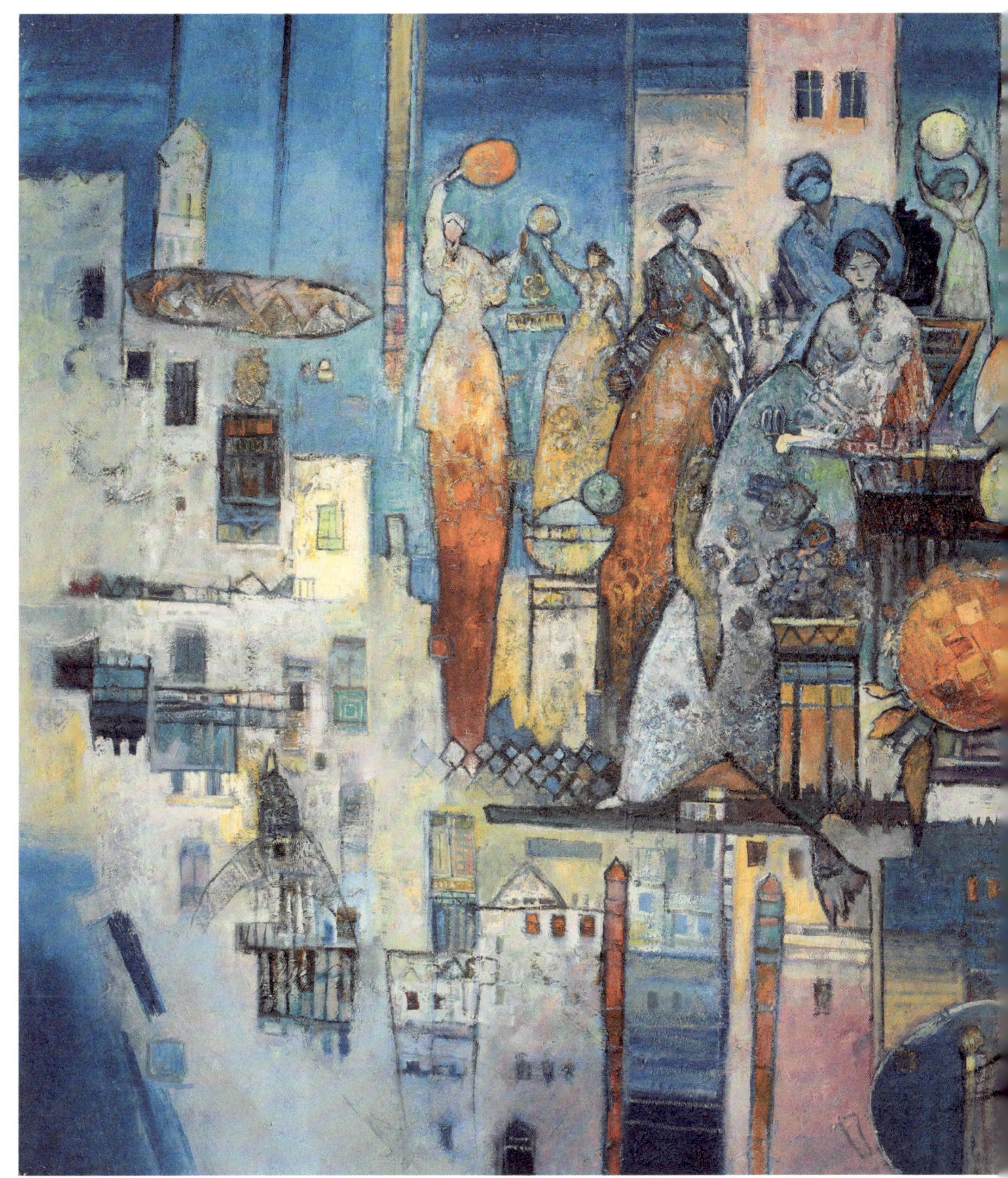

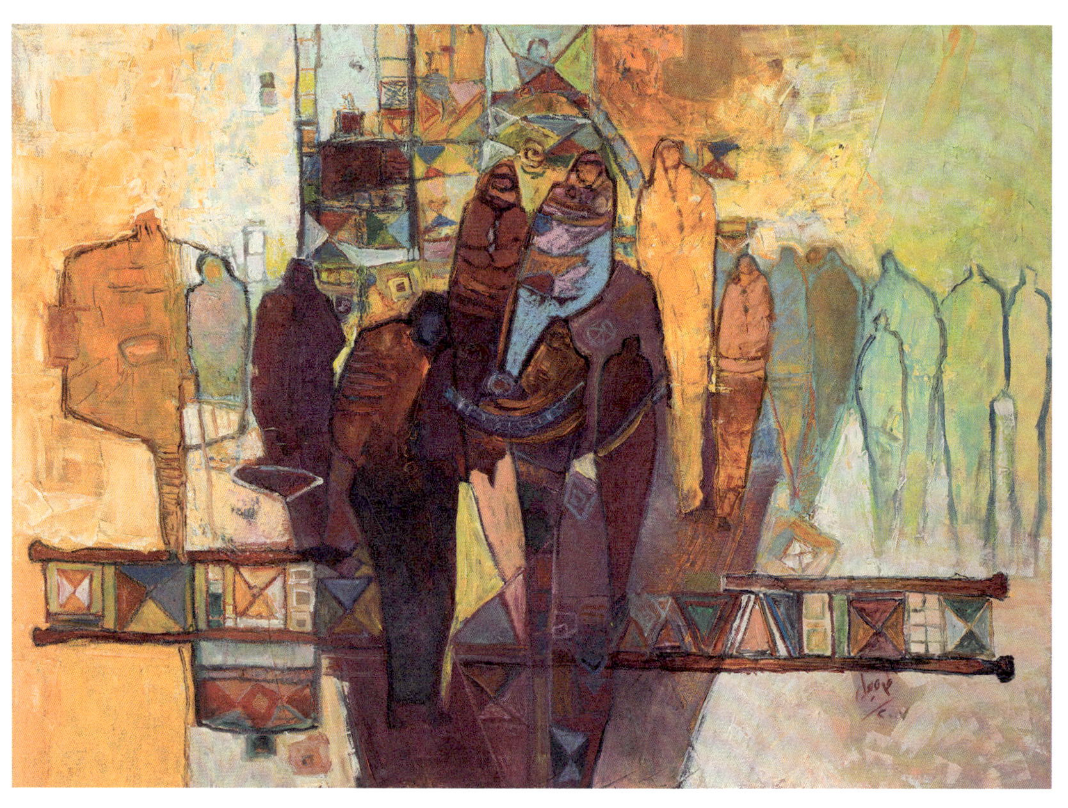

بدون عنوان، 2007

ألوان زيتية على قماش
76 × 102 سم
بإذن من الفنان

Untitled, 2007

Oil on canvas
76 × 102 cm
Courtesy of the artist

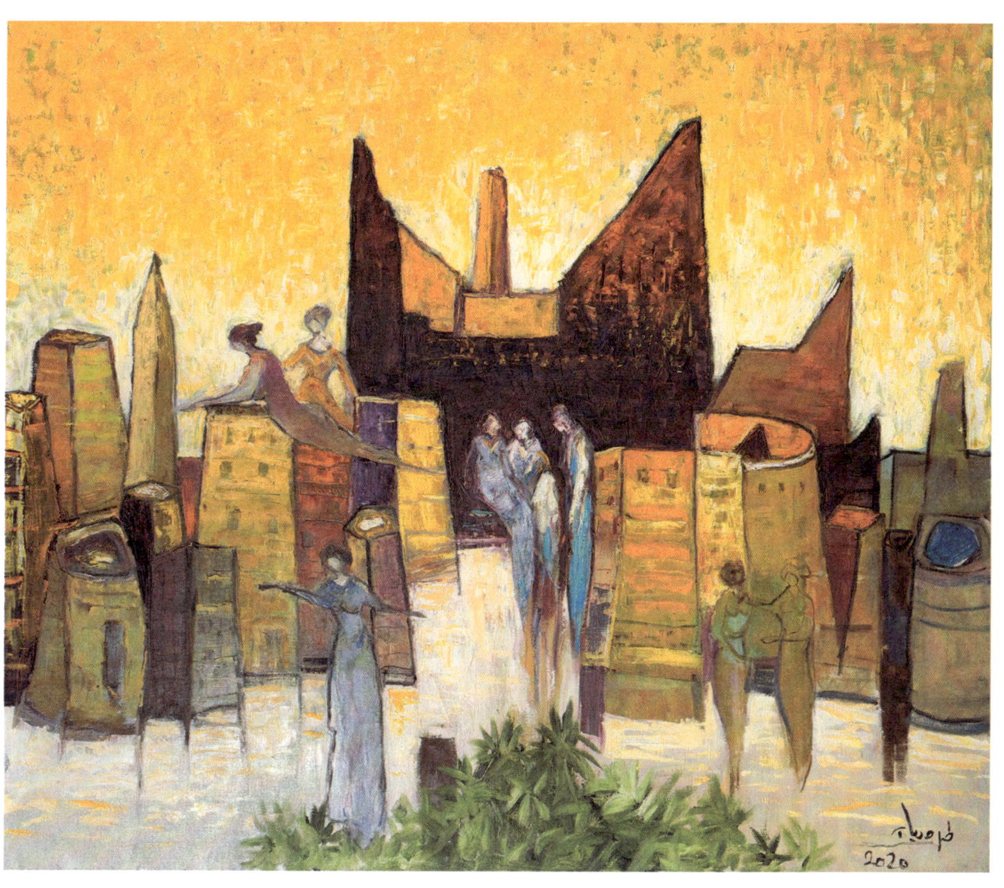

الدرعية، 2020

ألوان زيتية على قماش
160 × 140 سم
بإذن من الفنان

Diriyah, 2020

Oil on canvas
140 × 160 cm
Courtesy of the artist

Mares, 2019

Oil and sand on canvas
156 × 155 cm
Courtesy of the artist

فرس، 2019

ألوان زيتية وتراب على قماش
156 × 155 سم
بإذن من الفنان

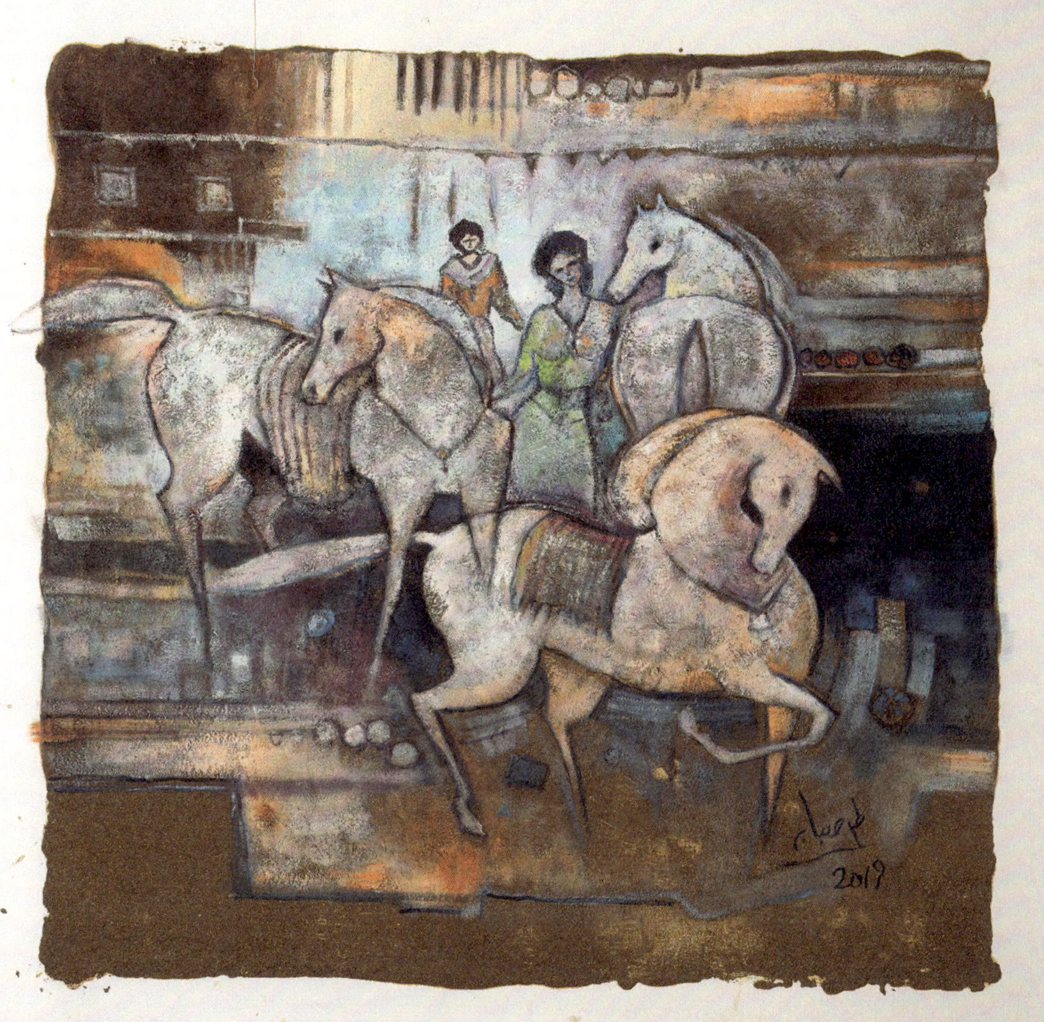

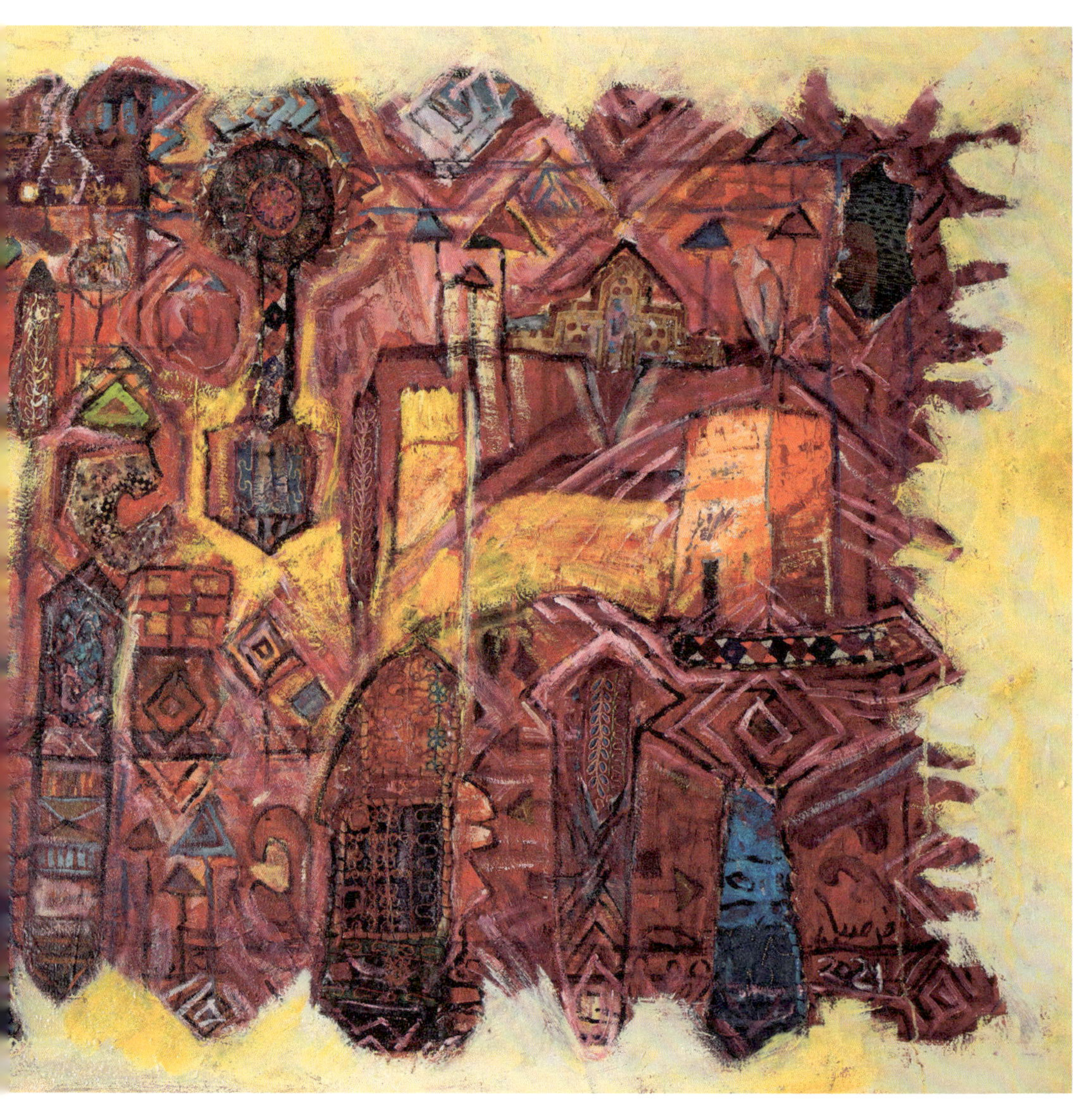

نجد، 2021

Najd, 2021

ألوان زيتية ونسيج على قماش
100 × 200 سم
بإذن من الفنان

Oil and fabric on canvas
100 × 200 cm
Courtesy of the artist

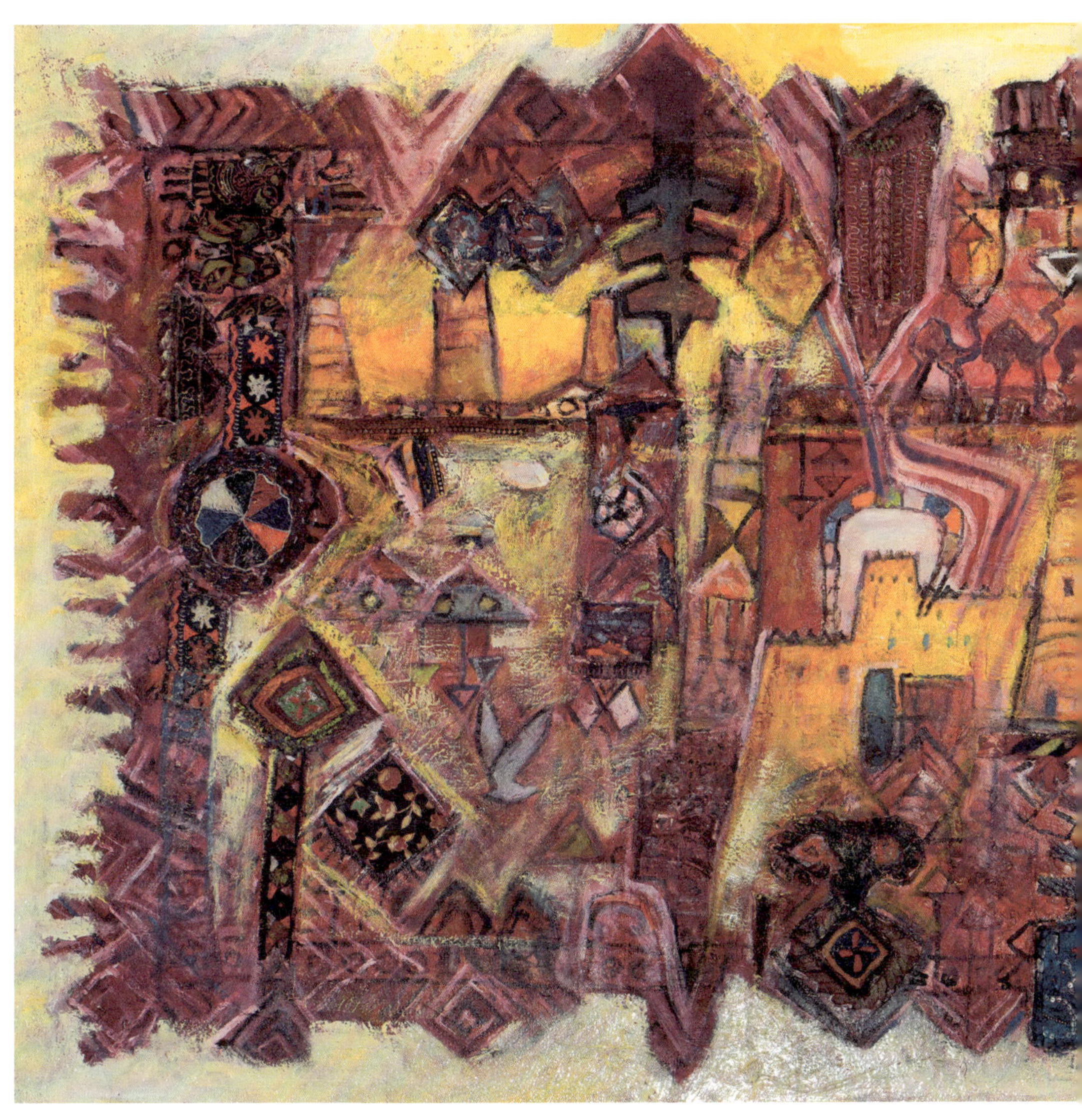

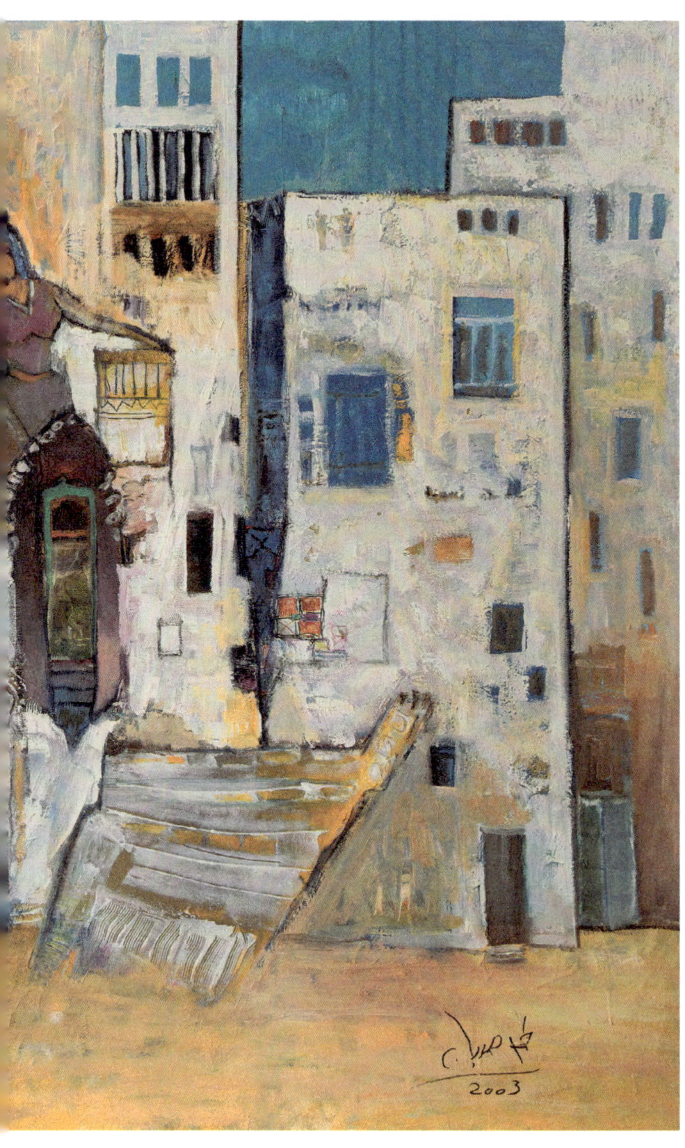

نساء في المدينة، 2003

ألوان زيتية على قماش
160 × 100 سم
بإذن من الفنان

Women in the City, 2003

Oil on canvas
100 × 160 cm
Courtesy of the artist

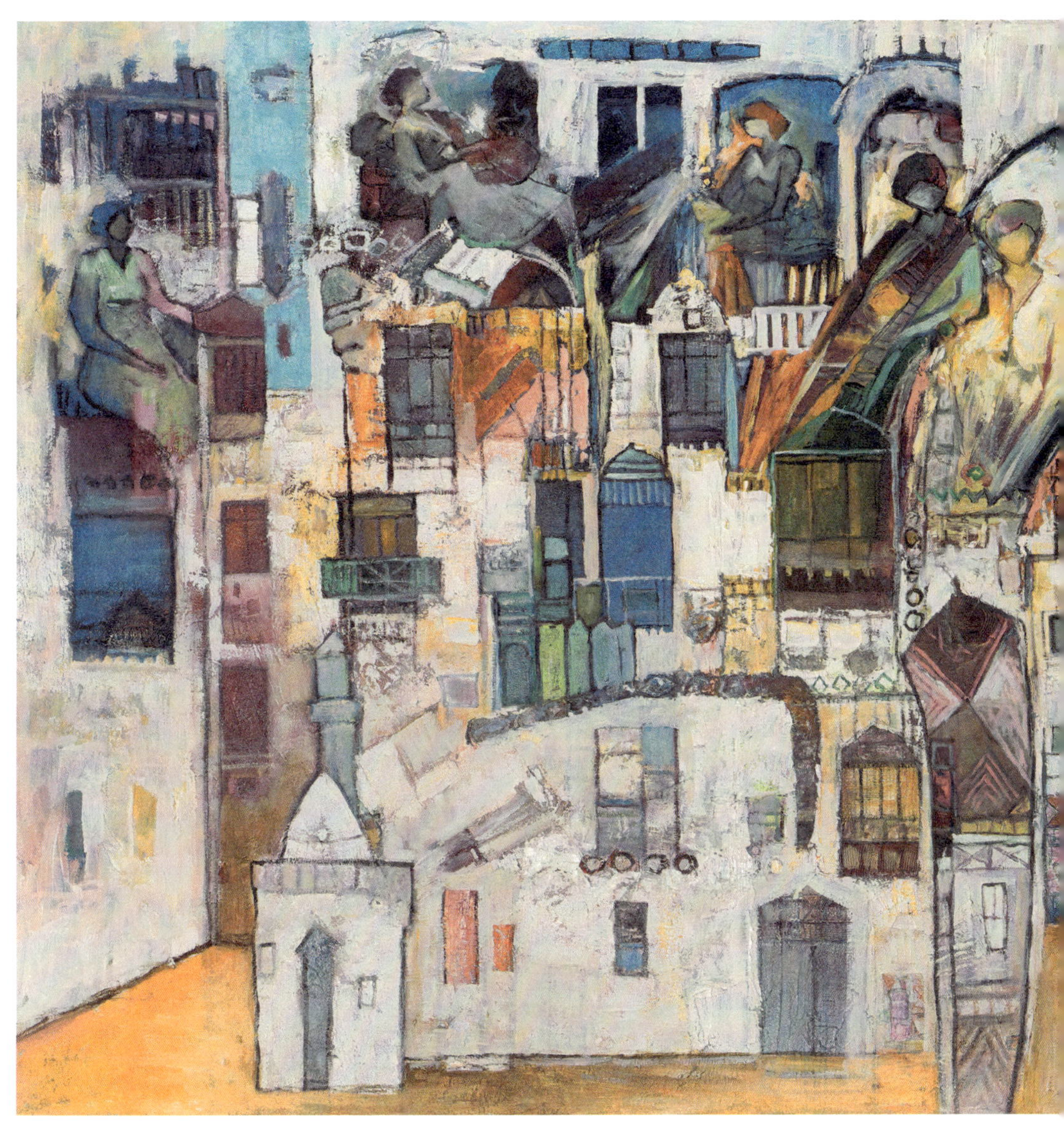

طـه الصبـان:
روح الأصالـة، بتعـبير التراث

Taha Alsabban:
An Authentic Spirit and Heritage Representation

أ.د. سهيل سالم الحربي، ناقد فني وكاتب أكاديمي
Prof. Suhail S. Alharbi, Art Critic and Scholar

Discussing the artist Taha Alsabban briefly may not adequately capture the depth of his artistic history, which spans nearly fifty years. Nevertheless, writing about artistic figures like him will always be an exciting endeavor. Although the works of Alsabban are well-known among artists and scholars, as I have addressed in "Depictions of Fine Art in the Kingdom of Saudi Arabia" (2003),[1] I remain committed to reading every available resource about him including interviews, personal conversations, and written materials.[2]

Through my research, I have been seeking for common themes to unearth new and unexplored perspectives about Alsabban. By delving into these sources, which encompass biographical accounts about his beginnings, his upbringing, and the influences of space and time upon him, I aim to provide a more nuanced and comprehensive understanding of the artist. Alsabban was born in 1948 in the historic and sacred city of Makkah, and one can ascertain that growing up in a city as rich in history and traditions as Makkah has profoundly impacted Alsabban and shaped his artistic vision.

الحديـث عن الفنان طـه الصبان قد لا يتناسـب مع تاريخـه الفني وغير كافٍ لاسـتعراض منجزاته الفنية التي امتدت لما يقارب الخمسـين عاماً، إلا أن الكتابة عن قامـة فنية مثله هـي دوماً مصدر إلـهام وإثارة، فعلى الرغم من أن أعمال الفنان طه الصبان معروفة ومألوفة لمتذوقي الفن والأكاديميين، وقد سـبق أن تناولتها في مؤلفي السـابق (عام 2003م)،[1] إلا أني استعنت بقراءة كل ما كتب عنه تقريباً، بالإضافة إلى مشاهدة مقابلاته وأحاديثه الشخصية.[2]

هدفـت مـن تلـك القراءات إلـى إيجـاد قواسـم مشـتركة، ومحاولـة تقديـم شـيء جديد لمـا يقال عن الفنـان، وإيجاد حـوار يجمع بين تلك المصادر لإعطاء صـورة أوضح وأشـمل عـن الفنـان، فالمصـادر والكتب تُجمـع علـى سـيرته الذاتيـة وبداياتـه، ونشـأته وتأثـره بالمـكان والزمـان، فهو مـن مواليد عـام 1948م ولهذا التاريخ أهمية كبيرة حيث من الضـروري للقارئ أن يعي ويسـتوعب شـكل المـكان. فنشـأته في مدينـة عريقة وقديمة مثل مكـة المكرمة لابد أن يكـون لها أثر عميق عليه، فلمكة المكرمة أهمية خاصة في الوجدان، وحتى تكون هنالك صورة بصرية واضحة، فهاتان صورتان لمكة المكرمة قديماً لمقارنتهما بلوحـات الفنان طه الصبان، حيث تظهر البيوت متراصة فوق الجبال المحيطة بمكة.

To illustrate the extent of the artist's influences, the two historical photographs of Makkah below can be compared to the paintings of Alsabban, where the houses appear stacked over the mountains surrounding the city, revealing a distinct architectural landscape. The houses in Makkah sprawl and rise along the slopes of its mountains, wrapping around its center and the Kaaba. These scenes evoke deep feelings of faith, ingrained in the artist's memory and conscience. Makkah's roads and winding *ziqaq*[3] alleys reflect the identity of the city, and its impact societally and economically, as the social bonds between its inhabitants are strong. The mountainous nature of Makkah influenced the layout of its houses, establishing a distinct urban pattern.[4] Building materials sourced from the local environment further contributed to the cultural character of its neighborhoods.

In many of Alsabban's paintings, Hijazi houses appear with these distinctive architectural features and characteristics, showcasing the visual aesthetics and color palette typical of the white houses of Makkah. His works were also inspired by the circular movement of the houses wrapped densely around the *Al-Masjid Al-Haram*, to the point of being adjoined, potentially bearing a direct influence on Alsabban's crowed compositions in the center of his paintings, contrasting to more spacious peripheral areas.

Alsabban spent many years living and working in Jeddah, a city that shares architectural characteristics with Makkah. Alsabban drew inspiration from its urban features and natural landscape. Living in close proximity to the sea, the artist was undoubtedly influenced. He incorporated the blue hues of the water into his paintings, imbuing its elements with the vibrant rush of waves and illuminating it with captivating lights that have earned Jeddah the reputation of a city that never sleeps. In some of his works, bold colors such as red and yellow,

فالبيوت فـي مكة تمتـد وترتفـع حتى سـفوح جبالهـا وتلتـف حـول مركزهـا وحرمهـا وكعبتهـا المشـرّفة؛ لتمتلـئ تلـك المشـاهد بالأحاسـيس والمشـاعر الإيمانيـة التـي تحتفـظ بهـا ذاكرتـه ووجدانـه، وكذلـك تتشـكل طرقاتها وأزقتها[3] الأمر الـذي انعكـس أيضاً على هويـة المكان وأثـر حضارياً واجتماعيـاً واقتصاديـاً، فالعلاقـات الاجتماعيـة في مكـة تتعـزز وارتبـاط السـكان بين بعضهـم البعض يـزداد صلابـة[4]، فالطبيعـة الجبليـة لمكـة أثرت في تشـكيل المنازل، حيـث فرضت نمطـاً عمرانياً مميزاً، ومـواد بناء مأخوذة من معطيـات البيئة، كما أثرت فـي تشـكيل حـارات مكـة المكرمـة وأحيائها.

تظهـر فـي العديـد مـن لوحـات طـه الصبان البيـوت الحجازية بسـماتها وخصائصهـا المعمارية المميزة، حيـث تشـاهد السـمة البصرية والإحسـاس اللونـي لبيوت مكة المكرمة البيضاء، كما اسـتمدت أعمالـه الحركـة الدائريـة للبيـوت والتفافهـا حـول منتصـف المسـجد الحرام، وتجـاور البيـوت حولها إلـى نان طـه الصبان سـماتها وطبيعتهـا، فتفجرت فـي لوحاتـه زرقـة بحرهـا فتشـربت عناصـره بزرقة مائهـا، فالألوان مندفعة كاندفـاع الأمواج الصاخبة، ومضيئة بأضوائهـا الجذابة التي جعلت منها مدينة لا تنـام، فتظهـر في بعـض أعماله الألوان السـاخنة كالأحمـر والأصفر ودرجاتهمـا، وينصهـران مـع بعضهمـا ويمتزجـان فيكونـان درجات لونيـة دافئة شـفافة كأنك تشـاهد شـبابيك الزجاج الملون لدور العبادة، وكأن الضوء يأتي من الماضي ليتلون بألوان الصبان فنشـاهدها كما نشـاهد الضوء المنبعث من الزجـاج الملون.

ظل الفنـان طـه الصبان تعبيريـاً بطبعـه، واسـتمد خصائـص المدرسـة التعبيرية فـي أعماله الفنيـة، فموضوعاته تنبع من داخله من أحاسيسـه ومشـاعره نحوهـا، وليسـت نقـلاً من عالمـه المرئي الخارجي، وإن كان تأثير المـكان قائماً، فمعيار تقييم جودة العمل الفني هي مشـاعره كفنـان وليس بناءً أو تكوينـاً أو قواعد وأسسـاً فنية، لذا فضربات فرشاته تتـم بتلقائية وكأنها تعمـل في اللوحـة باندفاع في

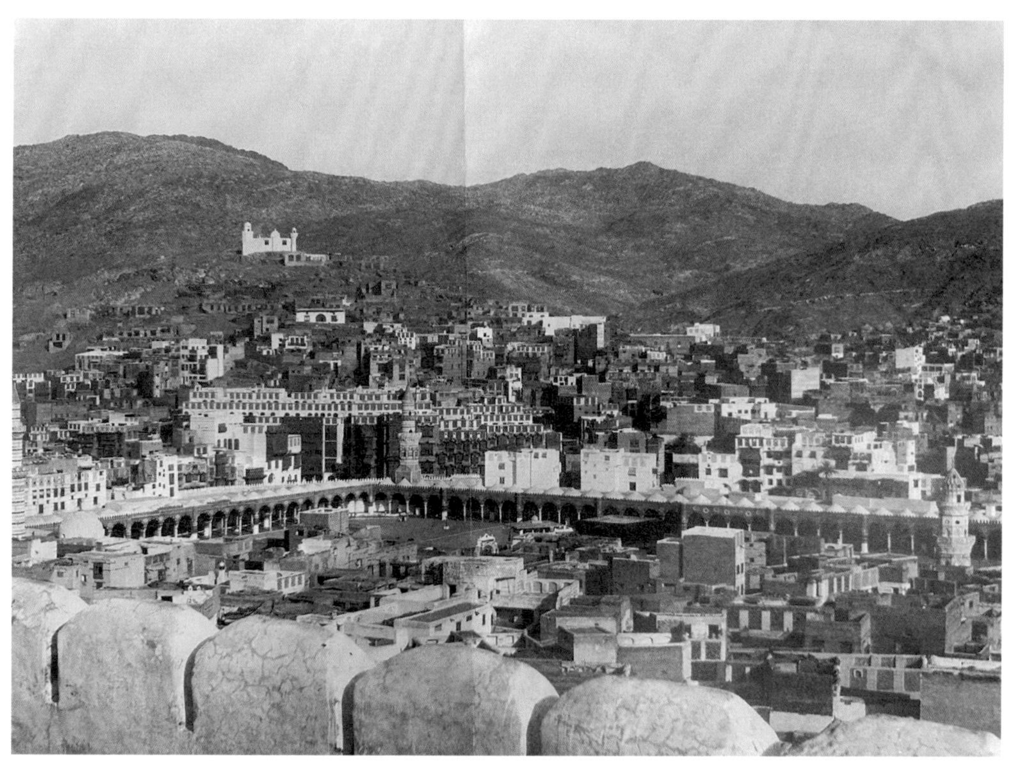

Makkah from the North, (1921)

Image retrieved from *Makkah From the Sky Past and Present*, 2015. Courtsey of the author

مكة المكرمة باتجاه الشمال، 1921م

كتاب مكة المكرمة من السماء الماضي والحاضر، 2015م

بإذن من المؤلف

Alsabban acknowledges the significant role women play in his life, particularly his mother. Being the eldest son among six sisters and one brother, and now having three daughters and a son of his own, women have always been a constant presence. Even when depicting the Hijazi architecture, which may initially seem devoid of people, there are individuals concealed inherently within the houses. A home cannot arise from a void, it is built through collaboration between men and women. Hence, in some of his works, Alsabban symbolically places women on the roofs of houses, representing their fundamental role as the foundation of a home.

In Alsabban's personal life, his wife, Mrs. Hayat, has played an essential role, serving as his first and most trusted critic. She actively assists him by participating in discussions about his artworks, while also providing input on their evaluation. Alsabban's daughters and sisters also hold great importance in his life, all of whom are reflected in his work.

At the core of Alsabban's interest and life are the different influential roles women play in society; as mothers, sisters, wives, and daughters. Alsabban strives to gracefully capture intimate moments such as the birth of his granddaughter. *A Mother's Love* (2013) is inspired by that deeply personal experience and depicts a mother embracing her child. In this artwork, women appear in traditional clothing standing proudly and calmly, imbuing the piece with a sense of tradition.

One may notice that the characteristic elongation of his figures mirrors the vertical architectural elements in his works as if they are in harmony with the act of prayer, where the movement of the head extends from the ground toward the sky. Human figures are at the core of Alsabban's practice, while

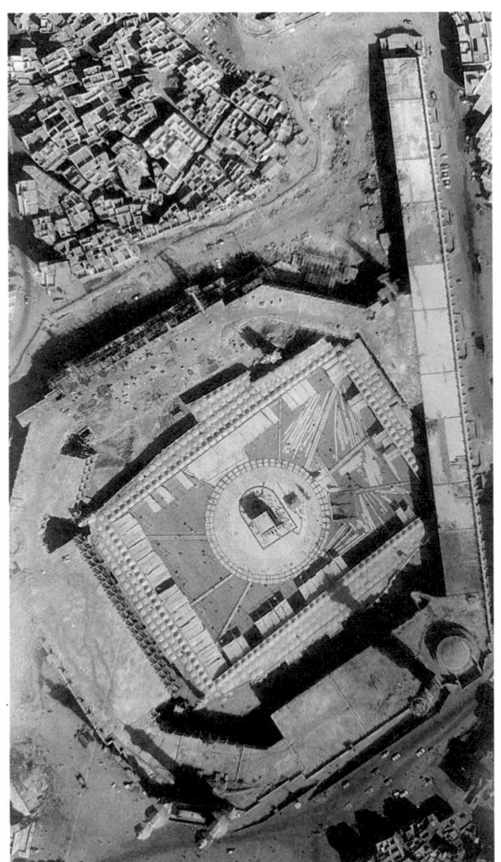

منظر جوي عمودي لمكة المكرمة، 1965م
صورة فوتوغرافية, شركة فيري سيرفي

Vertical Aerial View of Makkah, (1965)
Photograph by Fairy Survey

and their varying intensities, blend with each other in warm, translucent color tones, reminiscent of stained glass windows that can be found in places of worship.

Alsabban demonstrates an inherently expressionist nature in his works. The characteristics of the expressionist school are evident in his artistic process, as the themes he depicts emerge from within, conveying his feelings and emotions toward each subject. While place and environment may have influenced him, he did not simply replicate the visual appearance of the real world. His emotions dictate how he evaluates his paintings, rather than the construction, composition, or rules of art. This lends his brushstrokes a spontaneous, almost impulsive quality and an exaggerated manner. His subjects carry his emotional state, a longing for the past and its architectural imagery whilst contrasting with modern elements, including people and buildings. Alsabban combines a contradiction of place and time, infused with the spirit of authenticity and heritage.

Saudi artists have celebrated the female figure as a symbol in their artworks, and they are prominently featured in paintings either serving as a source of inspiration, being a central theme, or an essential component in the visual composition. Alsabban's portrayal of women serves as an artistic expression that reflects the social issues ingrained in the surroundings and cultural heritage of his upbringing. Rather than represent them directly, he intricately weaves these themes into his work through subtle insinuation and symbolic representation. Alsabban's themes possess an Arab identity characterized by the uniqueness of the Saudi environment. His paintings include rich colors combined with ornamentation and heritage iconography, lending them a distinctive identity and style that the artist has become known for.

أرجـاء اللوحـة وفـي أحيـان بشـكل مبالـغ فيها في بنـاء لوحاتـه وتصويـر موضوعاتـه التـي تحمل في طياتها حالتـه العاطفية المشـتاقة للماضي بمبانيه والمتفاعلـة مـع مـا يحيـط بعالمـه الحديـث مـن أشـخاص ومبان وسـمات جمعـت بيـن متناقضات المـكان والزمـان، وروح الأصالة بتعبيـرات تراثية.

تنـاول الفنـان السـعودي المـرأة كأحـد الرموز البصرية فـي أعماله الفنية التشـكيلية، مـا يدل على جاذبية ظهورها لدى الفنان السعودي، فهي حاضرة في أعمالـه كملهمة أو كقضيـة أو موضوع رئيس أو عنصـر مكمل أساسـي في بنـاء اللوحة بصرياً، وقد عبـر الفنان طه الصبان عن المرأة تعبيراً فنياً مرتبطاً بقضايـا اجتماعيـة ذات صلـة بالبيئـة والتـراث التي نشـأ فيهمـا، فهو عادةً لا يتناولها بشـكل مباشـر بل يضعها ضمن الإيحـاء والترميـز، فموضوعاته بهوية عربية تتسـم بالتفرد والتعبير عن البيئة السـعودية، فتجد ألوانه ثرية تمتـزج بالنقوش والزخارف التراثية ما يضيف إلى أعماله التفـرد ويجعلها بهوية ونكهة مميزة عـرف بها الفنان طـه الصبان.

يقـول الفنان طـه الصبان إن "المـرأة لها دور كبيـر في حياتي"، فوالدته هي من ربّته، لذا فقد تأثر كثيراً بها، وهو الابن الأكبر لسـتة من الأخوات وأخ، لذا فالمـرأة حاضـرة دوماً أمـاً وأختاً وزوجـة وإبنة. فحتى عند رسمه للعمارة الحجازية كانت تبدو بأنها بدون أشخاص بصرياً، إلا أن الأشخاص في دواخلها. فالمسكن لم ينشأ مـن فـراغ ..!! بل نتيجـة تعاون بين الرجـل والمرأة، لذا فالمـرأة موجودة في داخل تلك البيوت، وفي بعض أعماله يضعها على أسطح البيـوت كتعبير رمزي عن كونها أسـاس المنزل.

وفـي حياة الصبـان.. حياة، حيث كان لشـريكة حياتـه وزوجته السـيدة حيـاة حياة دور مهم فـي حياته فهـي الناقـد الأول لأعماله، وهي من يتـذوق معه العمـل الفنـي ويشـاركه الـرأي فـي أعمالـه الفنيـة وتثمينهـا، الأمـر ذاتـه ينطبـق علـى بناتـه وأخواته حيث يشـكلن جـزءاً مهماً مـن حياتـه، كل ذلك في أعمالـه الفنية.

collectively build the visual heritage in Alsabban's oeuvre.

Contemplating Alsabban's paintings, one might observe a variety of scenes that invite interpretation; one might see a girl in stride, or a bride amongst her bridesmaids, however, the details often merge with the background of the painting. One interpretation is that the ghostly presence of human figures serves a purpose in the compositions, allowing the artist to establish a symbolic connection between the illustrated people and their local environment.[7]

Alsabban has often presented an unidentified woman as a larger symbol of womanhood. Blurring and obscuring of faces is a distinct feature of his style, nevertheless, he conveys a range of emotions throughout his work. He portrays poignant events through the lens of individual characters—this approach is reminiscent of Aristotle's idea of tragedy—which may unburden emotions and purify sentiments. The works invite contemplation and allow viewers to engage and potentially be moved by their power.

In contrast, joy also holds an important space in Alsabban's works. He portrays scenes of women engaged in lively conversations and gatherings, where the ambiance is enriched by singing and music. These sounds are depicted as vibrant ripples emanating in the background, serving as a visual backdrop to women adorned in elegant and colorful clothing. The artist adeptly captured the essence of these scenes, inviting viewers to immerse themselves in the sounds and aromas, that feel palpable and emanate from the canvas. There is an inherent curiosity as to who might be truly listening in this vibrant atmosphere, where all the characters seemingly engage in animated dialogue.

In Alsabban's other paintings, which highlight women's dynamic roles, we catch a glimpse of women beating the tambourine in circular rhythms

فالمـرأة الأم والأخت والزوجة، مكون أساسـي في اهتمامه وحياتـه، لتضاف إليهـن الابنة لتجذب الفنان طه الصبان لحظات حميمية كلحظة إنجاب ابنته لطفلة، التقط الفنان تلـك اللحظة في لوحة "حنـان الأم" (2013م)، لتكـون محـور عمله الفني، حيث تنبض اللوحة بحنان الأم نحـو طفلتها وهي تحتضنها، فيما تظهر النسـاء فـي أعماله الفنية بزي تراثـي، يقفن بشـموخ وهـدوء يجعلان مـن العمل الفني قطعة تراثيـة متكاملة.

يـرى البعـض أن شـخوصه تتميز باسـتطالتها كاسـتطالة العناصـر المعمارية للمبانـي التـي يرسـمها، وكأنها تتناغـم مـع حركة الـرأس عنـد الدعاء، بالنظـر من الأرض امتداداً إلى السـماء، لذا فاسـتطالة المبانـي تمتـد مـن الأرض إلى السـماء، ويصف العنصر البشـري بأنه من العناصر المهمة فـي أعمـال الصبـان[5]، حيـث تأثر الأشـخاص لديه فـي بنائهـم بالعناصـر المعمارية، فتجدهم فارعي الطـول؛ تطـول أعناقهم عنان السـماء فـي التحام مع الأزقـة والحـارات، ليمتزجـا معـاً ويكونا نسـيجاً مـن التـراث والشـموخ والكبرياء؛ تلتصـق بعـض شـخوصه بل تندمج في العنصر المعماري للوحته ويكونان وحـدة معمارية واحدة تجمـع بين بنائية المـكان وزمانية الأشـخاص.

فتظهـر في عمله "بـدون عنـوان" (2020م) معانقـة ومقاربـة بيـن شـخصين، لا تـكاد تلمـح ملامحهمـا، فهمـا منصهـران مـع البنـاء والمدينة، ويظل تركيز المشـاهد على مركز اللوحة وسـيادتها، ليعطيـه الفنـان إحساسـاً بوجـود ملامح بناء في الخلـف، لتحمل بذلك شـعوراً بالالتقاء والاحتضان، فـلا يـكادان يسـمعان إلا نفسـيهما، ولا يريـان إلا بعضهما، هدوء وسكون حولهما، بينما هما يشعان حـرارة وحميميـة، وكأن اللقـاء كان بعـد فراق..!!

بعـض أعماله يتراءى بين الحقيقة والسـراب، بالـكاد تتبيـن تفاصيلهـا، وبعضهـا قـد ينصهر مع خلفية اللوحة، فقد تشـاهد كتلاً لونية، أو أشخاصاً من أزمنة بعيدة، وتتسـاءل أهو صمود، أم تقارب،

architectural elements play an essential role in their composition.[5] Hence, figures appear to lengthen their necks skyward, blending seamlessly with the alleys and lanes, weaving together as a fabric of heritage, nobility, and pride. Some of the characters remain distinct yet merge into the architectural elements and form a single architectural unit that combines spatial construction with the temporality of people. The merging of these elements can be observed across several bodies of works in various ways.

Using this perspective in *Untitled* (2020), Alsabban captures an embrace between two people, their features barely discernible as they blend into the architecture and the cityscape surrounding them. Yet, the viewer's focus remains drawn to them in the center of the painting. This composition gives the impression that the background is present but subdued, creating a sense of privacy and intimacy for the embracing couple—oblivious to their surroundings, they seem to hardly hear or see anything but each other, enveloped in stillness and intimacy, suggesting a meeting after a prolonged separation.

A sense of ambiguity prevails, in some of Alsabban's works, blurring the line between reality and illusion. Details are barely visible, with some elements blending with the background of the painting, color blocks or people emerging from distant times, and visions from memories conjuring happy faces melting into the past; all prompting contemplation on the inter-play between imagination and historical echoes. It has been suggested that Alsabban's characters seem to be drawn from ancient times.[6] Portrayed with a slightly formal aesthetics to evoke a sense of fiction and mythol-ogy, but he does not deliberately obscure details, as they take their form and objectivity from his imagination as well as from heritage in all its popular dimensions—storytelling, ancient tales, and life rituals—all of which

أم رؤى لخيـال ومـاض، فيما تبدو بعـض الوجوه فرحة سـعيدة في ذوبان مـع الماضي والذكريات.

يـرى المشـاهد أن شـخوص الصبـان تأتي من أزمنة قديمة دون أن تعلن عن تفاصيلها وجزئياتها[6]، فهـو يمنحهـا جماليـات شـكلية مختزلـة كأنهـا تخـرج من إطارها الإنسـاني ليلبسـها أجـواء خيالية وأسـطورية، وهو بذلك لا يتعمد حجب التفاصيل فهـي تأخذ شـكلها وموضوعيتها مـن مخيلة الفنان المسـتمدة مـن واقـع وإيقـاع تراثي بكافـة أبعاده الشـعبية في السـرد القصصي، والحكايات القديمة، وطقـوس الحيـاة التي تحولـت إلى مـوروث بصري لـدى الفنان.

تتأمل بعض لوحاته لمحاولة متابعة المشـهد وقراءته بصرياً، فهل تشـاهد فتاة تسـير، أم عروساً ووصيفتها، فالتفاصيـل تندمـج مع خلفيـة اللوحة لتظهر شـبحية الشـخوص أو الحضـور الشـبحي للقامـة الأنسـية، وهي مرحلـة تطلبتها ضرورة التأليـف، وربـط الأشـخاص بالبيئة المحلية.[7]

قـد تحتـار ..!! عندمـا تقـف أمـام لوحاتـه لتتسـاءل هـل الأشـخاص فـي أعمالـه حائرون أم نحـن الحائريـن..!! طمـس الوجوه وإخفاؤها سـمة لأعمال طـه الصبان الفنية. في أعمالـه الفنية يقدم عملاً لامـرأة مجهولـة، كرمزية للنسـاء، وكأنه يذكرنا برأي أرسـطو عن المأسـاة بأنها أثر فنـي، يصور فيها الفنـان الحـدث المثير للحزن في شـخص مـا، وهنا يظهـر دور المأسـاة في تنقية العواطـف وتطهير الوجدانيـات، عـن طريـق التأمل فـي العمـل الفني ومعايشـته أو الجـزع منه.

وللفـرح مسـاحة مهمـة فـي أعمالـه، يصور الفنـان طـه الصبـان مشـهداً لحديـث النسـاء وتجمعاتهـن لنشـاهد منظـراً تختلـط فيه النسـاء مع أصوات الغناء والموسـيقى التي انعكسـت على هيئـة تموجات لونية تنبعث خلفهن، تتزين النسـاء بملابس مزركشـة وملونة؛ اسـتطاع الفنان أن ينقل لنـا المشـهد الـذي تختلـط فيـه الرؤيـة المتعددة للألوان والأصوات الصاخبة مع إحساسـنا وشعورنا

known as the *burqa*. Women play important roles within the Saudi society and particularly among Bedouin communities. They actively participate alongside men in tasks such as tending to livestock, setting up and dismantling tents during travel, raising children, and managing household affairs, in addition to fulfilling roles specific to women. Beyond their practical contributions, Bedouin women also express their innermost sentiments through poetry, conveying emotions ranging from love, longing, and affection, to pain, heartache, and resilience. Women also appear in Alsabban's paintings within market scenes, showcasing their handcrafted goods made from locally sourced materials and tools or selling items such as clothes, jewelry, henna, or *kohl*.

Through these depictions, he captures the social dynamics of the marketplace, where women gather, engage in conversation, and forge new connections with one another. In a further exploration of Bedouin and local traditions, Alsabban's bases some of his paintings on Sadu[9] inscriptions. These intricate inscriptions are characterized by geometric shapes, such as triangles, rhombi, squares, and circles, which are rendered in the traditional Sadu colors of red, black, yellow, green, and blue. Alsabban skillfully dyes the characters of his paintings, allowing them to merge harmoniously with the background.[10] It can be observed that the Bedouin women with their distinctive costumes can barely be seen as Alsabban includes them amidst caravans and tents in desert landscapes. Alsabban's style can be likened to the transparency of glass, where the spectrum dances between the radiant glow of vibrant colors and the serene subtlety of muted shades.

Alsabban's artistic approach encompasses a variety of techniques. In certain works, he employs a blend of oil colors with translucent watercolor techniques

بروائح البخور والعطور التي تشتمّها بمجرد النظر إليهن، لتجد نفسك مبتسماً أمام مشهد يدعوك إلى الفرح والسعادة، وتتساءل أثناء حديثهن من منهن تستمع ..!!! فالجميع يتحدث ..!!!

بينما في لوحاته الأخرى، يقترب المشهد أكثر لإبراز فاعلياتهن فنلمح النساء وهن يضربن على الدف في إيقاعات دائرية ترقص معها العين متابعة لها، فتسير العين متنقلة في اللوحة يميناً ويساراً، لتخفف من حبكتها أزياء النساء الفرحة، فيما تظهر أحياناً رموز تستوقفك فتجد قارباً في اللوحة، وكأن الفنان وضعها لتزف العروس وتنتقل من شاطئ إلى شاطئ .. شاطئ أبيها إلى شاطئ شريك حياتها وعالمها الجديد.

من المؤثرات البصرية على رؤية الفنان وأسلوبه، زيارته إلى المنطقة الجنوبية مدينتي أبها وخميس مشيط، حيث تأثر بملابس المرأة في المنطقة الجنوبية بزخم ألوانها وزخارفها التي تزين ثيابها وما تحويه من خرز ملون ونسيج برعن في تزيينه، لذا ظهرت المرأة الجنوبية بملابسها المميزة في العديد من أعماله. بأسلوب تعبيري تعكس خصائص وسمات تلك النقوش الشعبية أسلوب الفنان طه الصبان وفقاً لما يشعر به وليس ما يراه، فالعمل الفني أقرب إلى الدراما البصرية التي تمتلئ بالمشاعر والأحاسيس، لتظهر لنا تعبيراتهن السعيدة وهمساتهنّ وأحاديثهنّ البينية.

وكسمة من سمات الفنان التعبيرية فلطه الصبان أعمال فنية يجمع بينها لون واحد، ومنها ما تسيّد عليه اللون الأحمر، على الرغم من أن دلالة الأحمر تتأرجح بين الحب والورد والشوق، وبين الدم والخطر والمنع، ويذكر أن التعبيريين اهتموا باللون الأحمر ودلالته في أعمالهم الفنية، فيما تكونت مجموعة أخرى من اللونين الأزرق والأخضر، لاسيما أعماله الفنية في بداياته[8]، إلا أنها تعاود الظهور بين الفينة والأخرى، وكما يقول الفنان عن نفسه وعن الأسلوب الفني الذي يستخدمه بأنه ليس مخططاً له مسبقاً بل يأتي بشكل تلقائي

in a manner that captivates the eye. The viewer's gaze moves across the painting, taking in the essence of women's festive joy. Occasionally, symbolic elements emerge grabbing the viewer's attention. For instance, a boat appears within the painting as if the artist positioned it to symbolize a bride's transition from one phase of her life to the next—from the shoreline of her father's to her new life partner's.

Alsabban's visits to the southern region of Saudi Arabia, specifically Abha and Khamis Mushait, had a great influence on his vision and style. There, he was captivated by the clothes of women, characterized by vibrant colors, decorations, and the embellishments of colorful beads and fabric. The southern woman and her distinctive attire became a recurring motif in many of his works. Alsabban's expressive style reflects the essence of these traditional garments not merely as they appear, but as he perceives and senses them. The works are imbued with visual drama, rich in emotion and sensation, conveying joyous expressions, hushed conversations, and shared moments between women.

Characteristic of the artist, Alsabban often incorporates a dominant color within his paintings, with a particular penchant for the color red. However, the associations of red vary, encompassing themes of love, roses, and longing, juxtaposed with notions of blood, danger, and caution. A notable collection features shades of blue and green, especially in his early artworks.[8] Although these hues reappear from time to time, the artist remarks that the colors and styles he uses are not premeditated, but rather arise organically and spontaneously. When reflecting on Alsabban's blue paintings, one may often find that they possess an allure that immediately draws viewers in.

Bedouin women are often depicted in Alsabban's works, identifiable by their traditional face covering

وعفوي، ومن يتأمل لوحـات الفنان الزرقاء، يجد أن الزرقـة فـي لوحاته لها ميـزة وسمة تجعلنا نندمج معهـا فوراً عند مشـاهدتها.

ظهرت في أعماله نسـوة من الباديـة تستطيع أن تميزهـن بما يرتديـن من غطاء للوجـه (البرقع). وللمـرأة فـي المجتمـع السـعودي عامـة والمـرأة البدويـة خاصةٌ مكانـة مهمـة في مجتمعهـا، فهي تشـارك الرجل بدورها البارز في رعي الماشية وإقامة الخيـام وإنزالها أثناء التنقـل والترحال، وتربية الأبناء والقيام بدورها في البيت، هذا بالإضافة إلى مهامها النسـائية الخاصة، بالإضافة إلـى أدوار ومواقـف بطوليـة وإنسـانية، فكـنّ يعبّـرن عـن مشـاعرهن بقصائـد وأبيات شـعر بدوافـع صادقة حباً وشـوقاً أو ولعاً وألماً وحسـرة، أو تفاعلاً وحماساً بالأحداث.

ظهرت النسـاء في أعمـال الفنان طه الصبان في السـوق وهن يعرضن بضائعهن مـن منتجات يدويـة استخدمن خاماتها وأدواتها مـن بيئتهـن المحيطـة بهـن، أو بيع ملابس أو حلـي أو منتجات لزينتهـن كالحنـاء أو الكحـل، فيمـا صـور الفنان طه الصبـان دور السـوق الاجتماعـي في تقارب النسـاء والتعارف وتجـاذب الحديث بيـن بعضهن البعض.

وفـي استكشـاف أعمـق للتقاليـد البدويـة والمحليـة، بنـى بعـض لوحاته بنقـوش السـدو[9] بأشـكال هندسية كالمثلث والمعيـن والمربـع والدائرة، وبألوان السـدو التي تصبغ بألوان طبيعية كالأحمـر والأسـود والأصفـر والأخضـر والأزرق، ليصبغها الفنان على شخوص لوحته بأسلوب فريد تندمج فيه النساء مع خلفية العمل[10]، حيث نلمح بصعوبة نسـاءه البدويات بأزيائهن المميزة، حيث تشـارف سـعير الصحراء والقوافل والخيام، فعالمه زجاجي شـفاف مثل أجنحة الفراشـات في وشـاح الأحـلام، وتتأرجح مشكاته بيـن وهج اللـون الحار ورطوبـة الظـل البارد.

يشتمل نهج الصبان الفني على مجموعة متنوعة من التقنيات حيث استخدم الألوان الزيتية بأحاسيس وتقنيـة الألـوان المائيـة الشـفافة فـي بعـض أعماله

channels his emotions into his artwork, allowing colors to evoke feelings rather than simply representing what he sees. In his paintings, elements are constructed without deliberate connection or intentional symbolism, except for their expressive significance. Alsabban prioritizes the exploration of personal expression over explicit meaning or financial gain, much like great writers, poets, and artists who do the same. He leaves the interpretation of symbols and connotations to the viewer, encouraging individual and subjective engagement with his art. By embracing intuition, emotional depth, and creative freedom, Alsabban's art invites viewers to embark on their own personal journeys of interpretation and self-reflection.

Endnotes

1   Suhail Salem Alharbi. 2003. *Fine Art Photography in the Kingdom of Saudi Arabia*. Alfan Alnaq Foundation. Riyadh.

2   This essay is an outcome of an interview with Alsabban 2024, among other sources.

3   *Ziqaq* is an alley, street, or narrow road that runs between houses and is usually winding.

4   Iman Abraham Kivi. 2015. *Social Life in Makkah during the Reign of King Abdulaziz Al-Saud*. King Salman bin Abdulaziz Al-Saud Chair for Studies of the History of Makkah.

5   Mohammed Kamal. "Taha Alsabban Colorful Memories." in Hisham Qandil. 2001 *Taha Alsabban Features of the Journey*. Arab Network for Publishing and Distribution.

6   Abdulla Idris in Zarban, Khairullah. 2018. "Taha Alsabban's Characters Converse" *Taha Alsabban. His life and Art*. Dar Almultazam for Publishing and Distribution.

7   Imran Alqaisi. 2007. *The Art of Taha Alsabban*. Dar Nelson for Publishing. Beirut.

8   Ibid.

9   Sadu weaving is a traditional craft of Saudi Arabia, characterized by intricate weaving of vibrant colored threads into geometric patterns, primarily associated with the Bedouin people but also embraced by diverse communities as a valued cultural art form.

10   Assad Oraibi in Hisham Qandil. 2001. *Taha Alsabban Features of the Journey*. Arab Network for Publishing and Distribution.

ليضفي عليها شـفافية في موضوعاتها ولتتناسب مع الإدراك الحسّـي والحوار البصري للفتيات. في العمل "بدون عنـوان" (2013م) أحب الفنان فتياته وأحب تصفيف وتجديل شـعورهن بنفسـه، لتثيـر فيه تلك اللحظة مشـهداً نسـائياً يجمع أربع فتيات.

والنسـاء في بعض أعماله بدون ملامح، ليضع المتـذوق صـورة مـن يـراه، ويُسـقط حالة اللوحة على الحالة التي يراها، فقـد يكـون جـزءاً منها أو تكـون جزءاً مـن قصيدة أو رواية قرأها أو سـمعها، فالفنـان طـه الصبان لا يصنع روايات مكتملة، ولا يميل إلى تسـمية لوحاتـه، بل يبقي للمشاهد جزءاً مـن المشـاركة الحسـية والوجدانيـة، ليكمـل معـه عناصر القصة.

لقد أثار التراث العمراني فـي الرياض اهتمامه، فعبـر عنـه فـي لوحاتـه ببيـوت الدرعيـة الطينيـة، واسـتمد مـن نقوشـها وزخارفهـا التراثيـة مـا يزين بـه ذلـك التـراث الفريد فـي خصائصـه، كمـا تظهر السـمات المعماريـة المميـزة فـي أطرافهـا العلوية والتي تتزيـن أشـكالها الخارجية بفتحات هندسـية تغطيها، وفي أعماله "نجد" (2021م) وضع طبقة مـن رمل الصحـراء كأسـاس للوحته، ثم رسـم عليها عناصـره الزخرفيـة وعناصره التراثية النجدية فيما يشبه السـدو بنقوشـه وألوانه.

خيـول الفنان طـه الصبان تلمـح فيها الأصالة العربيـة فتـرى جمـال هيئتها ورشـاقة حركتها وتناسـب أعضائها، فيما تشـعر بأنها إناث من خلال رقتهـا وأعينها.

والفنـان طه تقـوده اللوحة رسـماً وبنـاءً أكثر من أن يخطط بشكل مسبق لبنائها وعملها، فاللون هو ما يشـعر به وليس مـا يراه، والعناصـر تبنى في اللوحة دون أي رابط أو دلالة قصدية، سـوى الدلالة التعبيريـة، وربط الرموز والدلالات بينها وبين الواقع تركه الفنان للمشاهد، فـلا يكتـرث الفنان لذلك، وكعـادة العظمـاء مـن أدبـاء وشـعراء وفنانين، لا تعنيهـم الـدلالات والمعاني والنتائـج، بـل يتركون تفسـيرها للآخرين.

to give a captivating sense of transparency to his subjects. In *Untitled* (2013), the artist's fondness for the subjects is evident, he focuses on the intricate styling and braiding of girls' hair, creating an intimate scene that brings together four girls in a moment of camaraderie.

Notably, some of the women in Alsabban's work intentionally lack distinctive facial features, inviting the viewer to imagine the identities of these individuals. This intentional omission allows the viewer to project their own interpretation onto the painting, thereby situating the artwork within the context of their own experiences. Alsabban refrains from creating complete narratives or titling his paintings. Instead, each artwork serves as a fragment of a larger narrative, a broader story, or even a poetic composition.

Alsabban's artistic exploration extends to the urban heritage of Riyadh, with a particular focus on the clay houses of Al-Diriyah. Alsabban captures the essence of these dwellings, from the intricate inscriptions and heritage decorations adorning these unique structures to the distinctive architectural features visible in their upper edges. In his painting, *Najd* (2021), Alsabban employs a distinctive technique by using a layer of desert sand as the foundation for his painting. Over this textured surface, he then painted decorative elements and Najd heritage motifs, reminiscent of Sadu patterns and colors.

Apart from renditions of architecture and people, Alsabban's depiction of horses provides a glimpse into Arab culture. Their beauty, agility, and grace are palpable with their delicate features and expressive eyes, conveying a sense of femininity.

Alsabban's approach to painting, drawing, and composition is characterized by an intuitive and emotionally driven process. Rather than relying on premeditation, he allows his instincts to guide him and

المراجع

1 سهيل سالم الحربي(2003م)التصوير التشكيلي في المملكة العربية السعودية مؤسسة الفن النقي، الرياض المملكة العربية السعودية

2 مقابلة مع الفنان طه الصبان (2024م)، ومصادر أخرى.

3 الزقاق هو الشارع أو الطريق الضيق الذي يمتد بين البيوت وعادة يكون متعرجاً.

4 إيمان إبراهيم كيفي. (2015م). الحياة الاجتماعية في مكة المكرمة في عهد الملك عبدالعزيز آل سعود. كرسي الملك سلمان بن عبدالعزيز آل سعود لدراسات تاريخ مكة المكرمة.

5 محمد كمال.(2001م) طه الصبان ذكريات ملونة. في: طه الصبان ملامح من المشوار لهشام قنديل. الشبكة العربية للنشر والتوزيع.

6 عبدالله إدريس. (2018م) محاورةٌ شخوص الصبان. في: طه الصبان. حياته وفنه. لخيرالله زربان. دار الملتزم للنشر والتوزيع.

7 عمران القيسي. (2007م). فن طه الصبان . دار نلسن للنشر، بيروت.

8 المرجع نفسه.

9 حياكة السدو هي صناعة تقليدية في المملكة العربية السعودية، تتميز بنسج معقدة لخيوط بألوان واضحة في أشكال هندسية، وترتبط أساساً بأهل البادية ومن ثم تبنتها مجتمعات الفن كفن ثقافي قيم.

10 أسعد عرابي (2001م) في: طه الصبان ملامح من المشوار لهشام قنديل. الشبكة العربية للنشر والتوزيع.

<table>
<tr><td>

Muse's Reverie
Taha Alsabban

May 26 - September 19, 2024
Prince Faisal bin Fahd Arts Hall
Riyadh, Saudi Arabia

Curators
Aram Alajaji,
Assistant Curator at Misk Art Institute
Nada Alaradi,
Curator at Misk Art Institute

Art Direction
Amerah Altufail,
Art Direction Manager at Misk Art Institute

Exhibition Designers
Alanood Alkhaldi,
Exhibition Designer at Misk Art Institute
Badr Zabarah,
Senior Exhibition Designer at Misk Art Institute

Translations
Abdulrahman Sidi,
Senior Editor at Misk Art Institute

Authors
Aram Alajaji
Nada Alaradi
Prof. Suhail S. Alharbi
Basma Alshathry,
Director of Curatorial Department and Chief Curator

Copyediting
Ethar Alfaqeeh,
Copywriter at Misk Art Institute

Special thanks to the artist and his family
for their invaluable contributions.

</td><td>

عقيلـــة الخيـــال
طه الصبان

26 مايو - 19 سبتمبر 2024
صالة الأمير فيصل بن فهد للفنون
الرياض، المملكة العربية السعودية

القيّمون الفنيون
آرام العجاجي،
قيم فني مساعد في معهد مسك للفنون
ندى العرادي،
قيم فني في معهد مسك للفنون

التوجه الإبداعي
أميرة الطفيل،
مدير الإخراج الفني في معهد مسك للفنون

تصميم المعرض
العنود الخالدي،
مصمم معارض في معهد مسك للفنون
بدر زباره،
مصمم معارض أول في معهد مسك للفنون

الترجمة
عبدالرحمن سيدي،
محرر أول في معهد مسك للفنون

المؤلفون
آرام العجاجي
ندى العرادي
أ.د. سـهيل سـالم الحربـي
بسمة الشثري،
مدير عام إدارة التقييم الفني وكبير القيمين الفنيين

التدقيق اللغوي (اللغة الإنجليزية)
إيثار الفقيه،
كاتب محتوى في معهد مسك للفنون

شـكر خـاص للفنـان وأسـرته علـى مسـاهماتهم القيمة.

</td></tr>
</table>

Book Design and Layout
-scope Ateliers

English Proofreading
Zeina Assaf

All rights reserved. The reproduction of this publication in whole or in part, in any form by any electronic, mechanical or other means, including photocopying or recording or in any information storage or retrieval system, is prohibited without the prior consent of the publisher and Misk Art Institute.

First edition, 2024
© Kaph Books, 2024
© Misk Art Institute, 2024

ISBN: 978-614-8035-87-6

Printed in October 2024

Published by

ꝑKAPH

ART BOOKS FROM THE ARAB WORLD
كتــب الفـــن مــن العالـــم العربـــي

www.kaphbooks.com

Distribution
NORTH AMERICA - LATIN AMERICA - ASIA - AUSTRALIA
ARTBOOK | D.A.P.
75 Broad Street, Suite 630
New York, NY 10004
www.artbook.com

FRANCE - SWITZERLAND - BELGIUM - LUXEMBOURG
Les Presses du Réel
35 rue Colson,
21000 Dijon, France
www.lespressesdureel.com

REST OF EUROPE
Idea Books
Nieuwe Herengracht 11
1011 RK Amsterdam, The Netherlands
www.ideabooks.nl

MIDDLE EAST
CIEL BOOK DISTRIBUTION
Al Manara Road, Al Quoz 1, P.O.Box 282005
Dubai United Arab Emirates
www.ciel.me

تصميم الكتاب وتنسيقه
-سكوب أتلييه

المراجعة اللغوية العربية
محمد حمدان

جميع الحقوق محفوظة. يُحظر استنساخ هذا المنشور كلياً أو جزئياً، بأي شكل من الأشكال باستخدام الوسائل الإلكترونية أو الميكانيكية أو غيرها، بما في ذلك النسـخ أو التسـجيل أو في أي نظام لتخزين أو استرجاع المعلومات، دون الحصول على موافقة مسبقة من الناشر ومعهد مسك للفنون.

الطبعة الأولى، 2024
© كتب كيف، 2024
© معهد مسك للفنون، 2024

ردمك: 978-614-8035-87-6

طُبع في أكتوبر 2024

النشر من قبل

ꝑKAPH

ART BOOKS FROM THE ARAB WORLD
كتــب الفـــن مــن العالـــم العربـــي

www.kaphbooks.com

التوزيع
أمريكا الشمالية - أمريكا اللاتينية - آسيا - أستراليا
ARTBOOK | D.A.P.
75 شارع برود، جناح 630
نيويورك، نيويورك 10004
www.artbook.com

فرنسا - سويسرا - بلجيكا - لوكسمبورغ
Les Presses du Réel
35 شارع كولسون،
21000 ديجون، فرنسا
www.lespressesdureel.com

بقية أوروبا
Idea Books
نيووي هيرنغراخت 11
1011 RK أمستردام، هولندا
www.ideabooks.nl

الشرق الأوسط
CIEL BOOK DISTRIBUTION
شارع المنارة، القوز 1، ص.ب 282005
دبي، الإمارات العربية المتحدة
www.ciel.me